Also by Lisa Yockelson

THE EFFICIENT EPICURE
GLORIOUS GIFTS FROM YOUR KITCHEN
COUNTRY PIES

Wendy Wheeler

COUNTRY CAKES

———— ✧✧✧ ————

A HOMESTYLE TREASURY

Lisa Yockelson

ILLUSTRATIONS BY WENDY WHEELER

1817

HARPER & ROW, PUBLISHERS, New York

Grand Rapids, Philadelphia, St. Louis, San Francisco
London, Singapore, Sydney, Tokyo

FIRST EDITION

LIBRARY OF CONGRESS CATALOG CARD NUMBER 88-45909

ISBN 0-06-016092-6

89 90 91 92 93 DT/RRD 10 9 8 7 6 5 4 3 2 1

For Patricia Brown,
with deep appreciation

Contents

The women in my family always baked cakes that had a down-to-earth freshness and homey appeal about them. I grew up on these cakes and, over the years, crafted many, many more like them. Of the hundreds of recipes I have published in newspapers, books and magazines, the baking recipes have generated the most enthusiasm; many of those recipes are now in the hands of cooks across the country who are busy establishing their own baking traditions with them. I wish to thank all of my readers for their encouraging letters and their own tidbits of baking advice.

A book such as *Country Cakes* would be impossible to write without the support of colleagues and friends, talented—and persuasive—editorial guidance and all the expert people who turn a stack of recipes into a book you can open again and again. With very special thanks:

To Pat Brown, my editor at Harper & Row, for her strong belief in the importance of the American baking tradition, represented in the recipes that follow and in the companion volume to this book, *Country Pies,* and for her savvy food sense and style, which she imparted to every phase of this book's production; and to her assistant, Toni Rachiele, for her ability to watch over the manuscript like a mother hen and take so many changes and deadlines in stride.

To Susan Lescher, my literary agent, for her professional support, good humor and advice on the nuts and bolts of writing and publishing cookbooks; and to her assistant, Carolyn Larson, whose calming, reassuring manner made every crisis bearable.

To Joseph Montebello, Creative Director at Harper & Row, for his ability to take my collection of recipes and craft a glorious book out of them; and to Susan Derecskey, for her ability to edit the manuscript with the sensitivity of a cook and the skill of a writer, and for her professional friendship.

To Wendy Wheeler, the illustrator for this volume and the earlier *Country Pies,* for the line drawings and jacket illustrations that so clearly and charmingly bring my recipes to life.

To Lisa Ekus and Lisa Shanahan, publicists, for their expert help.

To the staff at Williams-Sonoma in Washington, D.C., for the generous amount of time and effort spent tracking down cake pans, loaf pans, bundt pans and many other kinds of baking equipment when my research demanded it; and to the staff at Kitchen Bazaar in Washington, D.C., for helping me find the good quality bundt and loaf pans used for many of the cakes in this book.

To Frank Randolph, interior designer, for the expert advice on the design and furnishings of my home, most notably the special attention paid to the details of my dining room, thereby providing me with a setting that always makes entertaining a pleasure; and to Jane Wilner, of Jane Wilner, Ltd., Haute Couture Linens in Washington, D.C., and New York City, for helping me select the lovely linens that have always graced my table settings, especially for my tea and cake parties.

To my longtime friends Lisa Stark and Mimi Davidson, for their encouragement and their ability to consume almost anything my test kitchen ever produced.

To Steven the Bear, for his support and dedication to all the projects I juggle.

And to my grandmother, the late Lilly Yockelson, who continues to inspire me in so many ways.

OLD-FASHIONED BAKING GOODNESS

Wendy Wheeler

American country cooking is sensual and forthright, lacking fussiness and rigidity. There's nothing quite like the rich textures and tastes of this homestyle kind of cooking: a well cured ham with its faintly sweet smell, a pot of greens simmering on the stovetop, jars of intensely colored peach preserves and raspberry jam lining the pantry shelf, the picnic cakes, coffee cakes, and keeping cakes—and those irresistible two- and three-layer cakes capped off with a good, homemade frosting.

Soft, meltingly tender cakes made from fresh butter, eggs, flour, leavening, spices, and not much more, conjure up childhood memories of happy days: birthdays, Sunday suppers, school or charity bake sales, holidays. These are the cakes that are a very special part of the American cooking tradition; they are vigorously flavored, simple to bake and easy to devour.

Country cakes are sumptuous everyday cakes, like a triple-layer coconut cake with a fluffy marshmallow frosting or a vanilla pound cake enriched with plenty of egg yolks, butter and vanilla; a gingerbread cake dotted with blueberries or a one-layer chocolate cake dressed up with a contrasting cream-cheese batter. They are especially pleasing served in the afternoon with tea or after supper for dessert. The cakes, made from dairy and pantry staples (which I like to call "goods on hand"), are made up of all the flavors we know and love. And most of the cake batters in this book can be put together in the time it takes to preheat the oven.

More often than not, the heritage of cake baking evolved from the tradition of a grandmother, mother or aunt who whipped up cakes on the side while the preserving kettle bubbled away or the bread dough was on the rise. Cakes were eaten almost as soon as they had the chance to cool off from the intense heat of the oven, and they never lasted much longer than the next morning, when farmhands or other early risers finished them off with a second cup of coffee.

The home baking that was accomplished by country cooks long ago was natural, effortless, direct—even though they had to contend with so many unpredictable elements, such as unreliable wood-fired ovens and less than foolproof leaveners. Still, all the right instincts of good baking endured and, with those instincts, heirloom-quality recipes; the recipes were then passed on to the next generation of young women, and the next.

My own lifetime of cake baking began in my paternal grandmother's kitchen, watching her make her now famous hot milk cake, or a white fruit cake or rich pound cakes baked in loaf tins. As soon as I was old enough to reach the kitchen counter, I took over the task of baking for our family and produced my first hot milk cake. This cake tastes of sweet butter, fresh whole milk, eggs and vanilla. It is the kind of cake you bake as a part of daily cooking, made as it is from what's on hand in the refrigerator and pantry. You can serve it by the generous slice with a hot cup of coffee or lemon tea or in wedges with a mound of berries and whipped cream. To me, this cake is the essence of country because it is sensible and wholesome, with a clear, pure flavor.

Other country cakes, tender and even-textured, contain generous amounts of spices, nuts, coconut or chocolate, and sometimes shredded or pureed vegetables, berries by the cupful or sliced ripe fruit. Cake batters are baked in tube pans (sometimes plain straight-sided pans, sometimes fluted ones), loaf pans, springforms, single-layer square pans, ordinary round layer-cake pans or muffin tins. Cakes might be finished off with a simple streusel crumble, a haze of confectioners sugar or a light and buttery icing. Many of the cakes in this book are delicious served as is; some of them just beg for a hand-dipped scoop of ice cream to be placed atop a slice.

The cakes in this book are the kind you would love to have at hand: a bourbon-laced pound cake to keep and slice as you like; a spicy apple cake to set out on the back porch midafternoon or evening and gobble up with coffee or tea; small vanilla cakes to serve warm, shortcake style, with sliced and sugared strawberries and whipped cream; a chocolate pan cake iced with a rich, thick frosting inlaid with chopped pecans—an easy sweet that can be transported in its baking tin to a neighbor's house, school bake sale or bring-a-dish supper. These are the cakes that never fail to please me, and I hope that the recipes for them find a permanent place in your baking file too.

THE SIMPLE ART
OF COUNTRY CAKES

*T*he smooth, almost rhythmic mixing of a cake batter is one cooking process that never fails to comfort me. Along with bread baking, it's cake making I turn to when I need to be reminded of the simple pleasures in life.

With only a few exceptions, the cake batters in this book are made in the following way: the fat, usually butter, is beaten for several minutes before a measure of sugar is added in stages and thoroughly combined; eggs and flavoring are then mixed into the batter completely; finally, a sifted or stirred flour mixture, which contains leavening and salt and any spices being used, is added to the batter alternately with a liquid, such as milk, buttermilk or cream. Sometimes the batter is further lightened with egg whites beaten to the firm peak stage, such as the cake batter in my Coconut Layer Cake (page 42), or further enriched with nuts, berries or chocolate chips. Occasionally, the batter is poured over an arrangement of fruit, as for my Peach Upside-Down Cake (page 82), Spiced Nectarine Upside-Down Cake (page 84) and Apple-Ginger Upside-Down Cake (page 86).

Cakes will emerge from the oven picture-perfect if you follow the directions to beat, cream, blend, fold or stir the ingredients together, as set forth in each step of the recipe. Generally, in the first stages of cake making, butter is beaten until soft and malleable; sugar is added, a portion at a time, then vigorously whipped into the butter; eggs (whole or just yolks) are beaten in, one at a time, to strengthen the batter and add volume and richness. After the flavorings are added (extracts, grated citrus rind, and so on), the flour and liquid are added. This final part of the mixing is done slowly and delicately. It is traditional to add the dry and liquid mixtures in alternate batches, beginning and ending with the dry (flour) mixture. This method creates the lightest, most even-grained cakes.

The yeast dough for my Caramel Upside-Down Sticky Cake (page 64) can be made in a large stoneware bowl with a great big wooden spoon and little else, except a good pair of hands for kneading the dough.

Some of the little cakes, such as the Ginger Cakes (page 130), Chunky Apple Cakes with Pecans (page 128) and Pear Cakes with Walnuts and Currants (page 138), can be made in one bowl, quickly and easily. In each of these recipes, a flour mixture is combined with a whisked liquid mixture to form a light, slightly lumpy batter. The batter is spooned into individual muffin cups and baked straight away. These cakes take minutes to assemble and well under 30 minutes to bake, so you can always have a little something sweet and fresh on short notice.

All of this, of course, leads up to the time when a cake is pulled from the oven, all fragrant and warm, and you just have to wait impatiently for it to cool before cutting away a big piece, even though no one has yet the chance to set eyes on it.

———————❖❖❖———————

THE COUNTRY CAKE KITCHEN

"Add a joyful touch of Grace!"

Wendy Wheeler

I enjoy filling the house with the sweet aroma of a cake baking, and I take pride in serving my guests something made from pure and wholesome ingredients. Since my first love in the whole realm of cooking is baking, I'm always mixing up some batter or another for big cakes and little cakes, dough for cookies and breads, crusts for pies. And I have amassed a pile of recipes and a load of bakeware, old and new, over the years. Still, I always go back to the dog-eared handwritten cake recipes that my mother and grandmother followed, and I continue to turn cake batters into the very pans that they used. The pans have a luster that only time and use can bring to them.

Baking a good old-fashioned cake, one that would make you proud, does not require an investment in fancy equipment or odd gadgets. Indeed, most cooks have probably accumulated much of the equipment listed here. I have listed the cake pans used in this book and the handy baking tools that are used constantly in my kitchen, all of which make the preparation of cakes a pleasurable experience.

Notes on equipment, ingredients and some of my favorite things

For baking, I prefer to use sturdy aluminum cake pans; such pans are readily available in cookware and department stores and in the bakeware section of most well-stocked hardware stores and supermarkets. Baking in aluminum produces layer cakes with an even-grained, light crumb, loaf cakes that rise high and moist and muffins that turn out plump, tender and well risen. What's more, aluminum pans are a breeze to clean up. I like bundt and tube pans that are lined with a nonstick coating and are well constructed. Look for pans with well meshed seams and tightly rolled edges. The best nonstick pans have interior surface finishes that are bonded on, not simply washed or sprayed on. I still grease and flour the inside of a nonstick pan before filling it with batter, for that little extra bit of insurance; this guards against small patches of cake batter fusing to the side of the pan—the work of a kitchen demon!

For cooking fragile stovetop frostings, such as the Billowy White Frosting in the recipe for Coconut Layer Cake (page 42), I use a good-size double boiler; it's made of ovenproof glassware and has remained in perfect shape for well over 30 years. If you don't have a double boiler, you can improvise one by placing a large, deep heatproof bowl over a simmering pan of water; just make sure that the bowl is anchored well over the pot so that it does not tip over.

A hand-held mixer will do a fine job of beating and mixing any of the cake batters in this book, although you must pick it up and put it down frequently, when you add a new ingredient or when you need to scrape down the sides of the mixing bowl. If you bake regularly, you will find that a free-standing electric mixer does the mixing, creaming and beating efficiently and quickly. A mixer whose bowl and beaters both revolve is the kind I would recommend. My mixer is equipped with both small and large bowls; the bowls, which are made of tempered glass, have straight sides and bottoms that curve gently inward. As the beaters beat whatever mixture is in the bowl and the bowl revolves, I can easily push a spatula around the sides to move the contents along; this, I think, is an important feature of the mixer. It may be my imagination, but I believe that this kind of mixer produces light, silky, even-textured batters and cakes that bake up high and moist.

Here are some of the small tools and bakeware I've come to rely on:

BAKEWARE

Three 9-inch round layer-cake pans

One 9-inch tube pan (about 4 inches deep, lined with a nonstick coating)

One 10-inch tube pan (about 4 inches deep, lined with a nonstick coating)

One 9-inch fluted bundt pan (3¾ to 4 inches deep, lined with a nonstick coating)

One 10-inch fluted bundt pan (3¾ to 4 inches deep, lined with a nonstick coating)

Two muffin tin trays (each tray holding 12 individual muffin cups; each cup measuring 2¾ inches in diameter)

One 8 x 8 x 2-inch square baking pan

One 10 x 10 x 2-inch square baking pan

One 8-inch round springform pan

One 8-inch round cake pan

One 9-inch round springform pan

One 10 x 3¾ x 3-inch loaf pan

One 9 x 5 x 3-inch loaf pan

One 9 x 13 x 2-inch rectangular baking pan

SMALL TOOLS

Dry measuring cups

Liquid measuring cups

Wire cake racks

Flexible metal and rubber spatulas

Measuring spoons

Waxed paper or parchment paper

Flexible palette knife

Nutmeg grater

Whisk

A country cake is made up of simple things—flour, fresh butter, spices, leavening and a flavoring or two. Once the pantry is stocked with staples and the refrigerator with some of the usual dairy goods, you'll be ready to make any cake in this book.

For cake baking, I like to keep a larder well stocked with ingredients, mostly because I love to bake and do so quite often. On the pantry shelf, I store bleached all-purpose flour, which I buy in five-pound sacks, and boxes of bleached cake flour. I have a supply of the sweeteners that I tend to use the most: granulated sugar, light and dark brown sugar, confectioners sugar and superfine sugar (a fine, almost powdery sugar, sometimes called dessert or bar sugar, available in one-pound boxes in most markets). I keep the flour and sugar in individual apothecary jars, sealed tight with their glass lids. Every few months I make up a batch of flavored sugar, such as vanilla sugar or lemon sugar, for flavoring and sweetening cake batters; I store those along with the other kinds of sugar. I also keep some confectioners sugar in an old glass shaker, so it is always handy for sprinkling over a freshly baked cake.

On another shelf, I arrange tins of baking powder, boxes of baking soda and numerous bottled extracts, along with jars and tins of ground spices, pouches of nutmeats, tins of sweetened shredded coconut and glass cylinders stuffed with plump vanilla beans and cinnamon sticks. I keep many kinds of chocolate—regular and miniature chips, bittersweet bars, squares of unsweetened or semisweet chocolate, unsweetened cocoa powder—on hand.

I always use fresh, not previously frozen, unsalted butter. Fresh butter is a delight to work with, and it creates a tender, fine-grained cake that rises impressively while baking. Butter imparts a full, rich taste to a cake. I use thick dairy sour cream, with no starch or preservatives added.

I buy all of my eggs, buttermilk and cream at a local health food store. The eggs are laid by free-ranging hens, and the yolks are thick and shiny, a brilliant yellow-orange color. I find these eggs indispensable for baking, sauces and ice cream. I buy both jumbo and extra-large eggs. Sometimes a batter needs the fullness of jumbo eggs; at other times, extra-large eggs are sufficient for binding and enriching the batter. Each recipe in this book specifies the size of egg to be used. (If you have only large eggs on hand, it's good to know that a large egg is equivalent to about 2 ounces or ¼ cup, an extra-large egg is 2¼ ounces and a jumbo egg, 2½ ounces. If, for example, a recipe calls for 4 jumbo eggs, you could substitute 5 large eggs. If you are making some of the big pound cakes and think you may be shy an ounce, it's safe to add an additional egg yolk to the batter. This works only for Best Vanilla Pound Cake [page 94], Bourbon Pound Cake [page 100], Spice Pound Cake [page 102], Rich Nut Pound Cake [page 104] and Cream Pound Cake [page 106].)

Good buttermilk is heavy and loaded with curds of butterfat, and the best kind is not treated to ultra-pasteurization or stabilizers. Look for dairy-fresh buttermilk at a local health food store or farmers' market, or best of all, a dairy that sells to the general public.

There is one last component of cake baking that is not a piece of equipment, and it is not an ingredient (at least not the kind you buy at the grocery store). It is the sometimes elusive "touch of grace." The poetic phrase, "Add a touch of grace," is repeated often in many old "receipt" books, frequently following recipes for breads and cakes. It is a reminder that baking should be done with a loving spirit. So, don't forget to add a joyful "touch of grace" to the recipes that follow.

———————◆◆◆———————

About cake plates

Be it sparkling patterned glass or richly colored porcelain, a beautiful cake plate shows off a cake in a wonderful way. Over the years, I've expanded my collection of pressed-glass cake-stands to include platters and plates, and I love to choose from the array of softly colored Depression-glass cake plates, flowery china plates and footed cake-stands, matching the cake to the serving piece.

Footed cake-stands, made out of china or glass, generally measure about five to seven inches high and range from nine to twelve inches in diameter. Most are finished decoratively with a narrow lip or modest fluted or scalloped edge that keeps the crumbs under control and prevents the cake from sliding off.

Antique pressed-glass stands known as doughnut or tea cake-stands are somewhat smaller, measuring about four inches high and seven to eight inches in diameter. These were made for serving such sweets as small, three-bite doughnuts, crullers, miniature cupcakes and little fancy cookies. Any cake-stand looks even lovelier lined with a lacy paper doily or flat, shiny leaves (such as galax or lemon) before the cake is placed on top.

A proper cake plate can range in size from nine to ten inches in diameter to a full twelve to fourteen inches. The larger plates are ideal for big, impressive pound cakes, such as Bourbon Pound Cake (page 100), Spice Pound Cake (page 102), Rich Nut Pound Cake (page 104) or Cream Pound Cake (page 106), or layer cakes. Smaller cake plates are ideal for fresh fruit cakes, such as Plum Cake (page 114), Spicy Apple Cake (page 116), Fresh Peach Cake (page 118), Blueberry Gingerbread (page 122), Peach Upside-Down Cake (page 82), Spiced Nectarine Upside-Down Cake (page 84) or Apple-Ginger Upside-Down Cake (page 86). Once the cake is positioned on the plate, I like to ring the edge with something fresh and pretty, like sprigs of lavender or heather or cherry, apple or peach blossoms.

BACK PORCH
CAKES

Wendy Wheeler

BACK PORCH CAKES

———◆◆◆———

Marbled German Chocolate Cake   32
Black Walnut and Chocolate Pan Cake   34
Orange Cake   36
Buttermilk Cake   38
Buttermilk Chocolate Layer Cake   40
Coconut Layer Cake   42

Relaxing on the back porch (or veranda or patio) with a piece of cake and a hot or cold drink is just the thing to do when the living is easy. The porch with its washed pine, wicker or painted furniture is also the place for the time-honored rituals of shucking corn and cranking the ice-cream maker.

Cakes to be savored midafternoon with a cup of tea should be informal, plain and rather buttery. For those times, cut into a freshly baked Orange Cake (page 36), Buttermilk Cake (page 38) or Black Walnut and Chocolate Pan Cake (page 34). Reserve the tall iced layer cakes and the fudgy, cheesecake-based Marbled German Chocolate Cake (page 32) for well after dinner, when there's time to linger over and appreciate a toothsome dessert. A pot of hot coffee or a pitcher of iced tea, depending on the weather and your mood, should be served along with the cake.

Back porch cakes look particularly appealing, I think, when presented on old pressed-glass cake-stands or flat, flowery cake plates. Mostly, I use the plates and stands from my collection of Depression glass; the pink-, green- or amber-hued plates seem to show off pieces of cake gloriously. Since the big layer cakes cut into deep, hefty slices, I serve those on large luncheon or dinner plates; smaller dishes can handle daintier cakes.

Marbled German Chocolate Cake

FOR THE CREAM CHEESE MIXTURE:

6 ounces cream cheese, softened at room temperature

4 tablespoons (½ stick) unsalted butter, softened at room temperature

⅓ cup granulated sugar

2 extra-large eggs, at room temperature

2 tablespoons plus 2 teaspoons *sifted* cake flour

2 teaspoons pure vanilla extract

FOR THE GERMAN CHOCOLATE CAKE BATTER:

8 ounces (2 bars) German's sweet chocolate, coarsely chopped

½ cup (1 stick) unsalted butter, cut in chunks

1 cup *unsifted* cake flour

This flavorful square cake is a swirled blend of rich vanilla cheesecake and mellow German chocolate cake. The waves of cheesecake keep the whole cake moist and make each bite taste creamy and silky. My mother baked a Marbled German Chocolate Cake nearly every Saturday morning to serve over the weekend. This is my version of her cake.

Small squares or thick fingers of this cake are delicious served with tall glasses of iced coffee made from freshly ground coffee beans. I serve a little pot of cream and a bowl of superfine sugar with iced coffee.

———❖❖❖———

Lightly butter and flour a 10-inch square baking pan; set aside. Preheat the oven to 350 degrees.

For the cream cheese mixture, beat the cream cheese and butter in the small bowl of an electric mixer on moderately high speed for 2 minutes. Beat in the sugar. Blend in the eggs, one at a time, beating well after each one. Add the flour and blend it in on low speed. Blend in the vanilla; set aside. Wash and dry the beaters.

For the German chocolate cake batter, melt the chopped chocolate and butter chunks in a small heavy saucepan over low heat. When the chocolate and butter have melted down completely, remove the saucepan from the heat and stir once or twice; set aside.

Sift together the flour, baking powder and salt onto a sheet of waxed paper. Beat the eggs in the large bowl of an

½ teaspoon baking
 powder

½ teaspoon salt

4 extra-large eggs, at
 room temperature

1¼ cups Vanilla-Scented
 Granulated Sugar
 (page 95) or plain
 granulated sugar

2 teaspoons pure vanilla
 extract

One 10-inch square cake

electric mixer on moderate speed for 1 minute. Beat in the sugar and vanilla. With the mixer on low speed, blend in the chocolate-butter mixture until combined. Add the sifted dry ingredients in 2 additions, beating just until the particles of flour have been absorbed.

Pour two-thirds of the German chocolate cake batter into the prepared baking pan. Spoon the cream cheese batter on top. Carefully pour the remaining German chocolate cake batter on top of that. Using a plain table knife, marbleize the batters by drawing the knife through all 3 layers in gentle swirls.

Bake the cake on the lower-third-level rack of the pre-heated oven for 40 to 45 minutes, or until a wooden pick inserted in the center of the cake comes out almost clean (a few moist particles will still cling) and the cake pulls slightly away from the sides of the pan.

Let the cake cool in the pan on a wire rack for 10 minutes. Carefully invert the pan onto a second rack, then invert again to cool right side up.

Serve the cake cut in fingers or squares.

Black Walnut and Chocolate Pan Cake

4 ounces (4 squares) unsweetened chocolate, roughly chopped

1 cup (2 sticks) unsalted butter, cut in chunks

1½ cups *unsifted* cake flour

¼ teaspoon baking powder

½ teaspoon salt

4 jumbo eggs, at room temperature

2 cups Vanilla-Scented Granulated Sugar (page 95)

2 teaspoons pure vanilla extract

1 cup chopped black walnuts

Confectioners sugar for dusting (optional)

One 9-inch round cake

A fudge cake with body and substance, this is best served in thin wedges. The fine, full aroma of chocolate comes through in each slice, as does the distinctive flavor of black walnuts. A scoop of Pure Vanilla Ice Cream (page 142) would make a lovely accompaniment to a slice of this cake, as its subtle, understated taste plays nicely against the deep, dark flavor of the chocolate. Any leftover cake can be broken up into little chunks, mashed slightly with the back of a knife or cleaver and folded into softened vanilla ice cream. The brownie-like bits become embedded in the ice cream. It's a concoction everyone seems to like.

Lightly butter a 9-inch round springform pan. Line the bottom of the pan with a round of waxed paper. Dust the sides of the pan with flour; set aside. Preheat the oven to 375 degrees.

Place the chocolate and butter in a medium-size saucepan, set over low heat and cook slowly until the butter and chocolate have melted down completely. Set aside to cool.

Stir together the flour, baking powder and salt in a small bowl. Place the eggs in the large bowl of an electric mixer and beat on high speed for 30 seconds. Add the sugar and beat for 30 seconds longer. By hand, whisk together the chocolate-butter mixture and vanilla for a few seconds, then add it to the eggs and sugar. Beat on low speed until the chocolate mixture is incorporated. By hand, stir in the flour, beating slowly with a wooden spoon just until the particles of flour have been absorbed. Fold in half of the walnuts. Spoon the batter into the prepared pan. Spread the batter evenly in the pan. Sprinkle the remaining walnuts evenly over the top.

Bake the cake on the lower-third-level rack of the preheated oven for 45 minutes, or until a wooden pick inserted in the center of the cake comes out barely clean; the cake will just begin to pull away from the sides of the pan.

Let the cake cool in the pan on a wire rack for 30 minutes. Remove the outside hinged ring of the pan and let the cake cool completely. When it has reached room temperature (about 4 to 5 hours), invert it onto a second cooling rack, then invert again so that the cake is right side up. Sift a little confectioners sugar over the top, if you like.

Serve the cake cut in narrow wedges.

Orange Cake

3½ cups *unsifted* all-
purpose flour

1 tablespoon hot water

½ teaspoon baking soda

1 cup buttermilk, at
room temperature

1 cup shortening

½ cup (1 stick) unsalted
butter, softened at
room temperature

2½ cups granulated
sugar

4 jumbo eggs, at room
temperature

1 tablespoon pure
orange extract

1 tablespoon finely
grated orange rind

1 tablespoon orange
liqueur, such as
Cointreau, Grand
Marnier or Triple Sec

FOR THE ORANGE GLAZE:

2 tablespoons finely
julienned orange peel
(see Note)

½ cup freshly squeezed
orange juice

Orange extract, grated orange rind and orange liqueur perfume this big cake with a heady citrus fragrance. The cake,
still warm from the oven, is crowned with a glaze containing
thin wisps of orange rind. Pair slices of Orange Cake with a
pot of Darjeeling tea for a revitalizing midafternoon treat. I
have this special recipe from my good friend Mimi Davidson, who created the cake for a local restaurant several years
ago. Mimi likes to have one on hand for weekend guests.

Lightly butter and flour a 10-inch fluted bundt pan; set
aside. Preheat the oven to 350 degrees.

Sift the flour onto a sheet of waxed paper; set aside.

Place the hot water in a small bowl, add the baking soda
and stir to dissolve. Whisk the baking soda mixture into the
buttermilk and set aside.

Cream the shortening and butter in the large bowl of an
electric mixer on moderately high speed for 3 minutes. Add
the sugar in 3 additions, beating thoroughly on moderate
speed until light and white-looking after each portion is
added. Beat in the eggs, one at a time, beating thoroughly
after each one. Scrape down the sides of the mixing bowl
often to keep the mixture even-textured. With the mixer on
low speed, alternately add the flour in 3 additions and the
buttermilk in 2 additions, beginning and ending with flour.
Beat in the orange extract, orange rind and orange liqueur.
Pour and scrape the batter into the prepared pan. Shake
the pan gently from side to side to level the top of the batter.

¾ cup granulated sugar

1½ teaspoons water

1 tablespoon orange liqueur (the same as that used in the cake batter)

One 10-inch bundt cake

Bake the cake on the lower-third-level rack of the preheated oven for 1 hour and 20 minutes to 1 hour and 30 minutes, or until a wooden pick inserted into the middle of the cake comes out clean and dry and the cake pulls away slightly from the edges of the pan.

While the cake is baking, make the orange glaze. Put the orange peel in a small saucepan of boiling water; boil 1 minute. Drain the peel in a small stainless steel sieve and refresh it under cold running water. Drain on paper toweling. Place the peel, orange juice, sugar, water and liqueur in a medium-size stainless steel or enameled cast-iron saucepan. Cover the pan and set over low heat; cook slowly until the sugar has dissolved completely. When every last granule of sugar has melted down, uncover the pot and bring the contents of the saucepan to the boil. Boil for 3 minutes and remove from the heat.

Let the cake cool in the pan on a wire rack for 5 minutes. Spoon a third of the syrup (without any peel) over the cake while it is still in the pan. When the syrup has been absorbed, carefully invert the cake onto a second cooling rack. Spoon the remaining syrup, along with the wisps of peel, over the top. Let cool completely.

Serve the cake cut in medium thick slices.

Note: To make finely julienned orange peel, pare long, wide strips from the outer peel of a thick-skinned orange (like a navel orange), square off the ends with a sharp knife, then cut ¹⁄₁₆-inch-wide strips from the sections of peel.

Buttermilk Cake

1 tablespoon finely
   grated lemon rind

1 tablespoon plus
   1 teaspoon pure
   lemon extract

3½ cups *sifted* all-
   purpose flour

¼ teaspoon salt

½ teaspoon baking soda

1 cup buttermilk, at
   room temperature

1½ cups (3 sticks)
   unsalted butter,
   softened at room
   temperature

2½ cups granulated
   sugar

5 jumbo eggs, at room
   temperature

FOR THE LEMON GLAZE:

⅓ cup freshly squeezed
   and strained lemon
   juice

¾ cup granulated sugar

One 10-inch bundt cake

The cool and tart flavor of lemon peel adds a zesty—and graceful—note to this cake. I like to let the finely grated lemon peel steep in an ample amount of lemon extract well before it is beaten into the batter, so that the peel has the chance to bloom. The lemon glaze is a nice finishing touch, adding as it does a feather-light sweet-and-sour coating. Thick hunks of Buttermilk Cake are wonderful served in summer with piles of fresh berries and mounds of whipped cream. Slender slices of cake, perhaps two to a serving, served with a warm compote of dried fuit, make a marvelous midwinter treat.

———◆◆◆———

Lightly butter and flour a 10-inch fluted bundt pan; set aside. Preheat the oven to 350 degrees.

Blend the lemon rind and lemon extract together in a small cup; set aside.

Sift together the flour and salt onto a sheet of waxed paper; set aside. Stir the baking soda into the buttermilk; set aside.

Cream the butter in the large bowl of an electric mixer on moderately high speed for 3 minutes. Add the sugar in 3 additions, beating for 1 minute on moderately high speed after each portion is added. Beat in the eggs, one at a time, blending well after each addition. Blend in the lemon rind–extract mixture. Scrape down the sides of the mixing bowl to keep the mixture even-textured. With the mixer on low speed, alternately add the flour in 3 additions with the buttermilk in 2 additions, beginning and ending with flour. Pour and scrape the batter into the prepared pan.

Bake the cake on the lower third level rack of the pre-heated oven for about 1 hour and 15 minutes, or until a wooden pick inserted in the center of the cake comes out clean and dry and the cake pulls away slightly from the edges of the pan.

Let the cake cool in the pan on a wire rack for 5 minutes.

To make the glaze, combine the lemon juice and sugar in a small bowl. Invert the cake onto a second cooling rack. Brush the glaze over the top and sides of the hot cake. Let cool completely.

Serve the cake cut in thin slices.

Buttermilk Chocolate Layer Cake

2 cups *sifted* cake flour

1½ teaspoons baking soda

¼ teaspoon salt

½ cup (1 stick) unsalted butter, softened at room temperature

1½ cups granulated sugar

2 extra-large eggs, at room temperature

1 teaspoon pure vanilla extract

3 ounces (3 squares) unsweetened chocolate, melted and cooled

1½ cups buttermilk, at room temperature

FOR THE THIN AND RICH CHOCOLATE FROSTING:

3 ounces (3 squares) unsweetened chocolate, coarsely chopped

A chocolate layer cake as fine-grained and light as this is typical of the kind you would meet up with at a county fair, church supper or neighborhood get-together. It is beloved for its intense chocolate flavor, ethereal texture and rich frosting. This is a good cake to have around to satisfy the teatime sweet tooth. I like to assemble the cake on a pressed-glass cake-stand lined with doilies and serve big pieces on glass plates in the same pattern as the stand.

———❖❖❖———

Lightly butter and flour the inside of two 9-inch round cake pans. Line the bottom of each pan with a circle of waxed paper; set aside. Preheat the oven to 350 degrees.

Resift the flour with the baking soda and salt onto a large sheet of waxed paper. Cream the butter in the large bowl of an electric mixer on moderate speed for 3 minutes. Beat in the sugar in 2 additions, beating well after each portion is added. Beat in the eggs, one at a time, blending well after each one. Blend in the vanilla and melted chocolate and beat on low speed until the mixture is chocolate colored throughout, scraping down the sides of the bowl with a rubber spatula to keep the mixture even-textured. With the mixer on low speed, alternately add the sifted flour mixture in 3 additions and the buttermilk in 2 additions, beginning and ending with the flour mixture. Pour and scrape the batter into the prepared pans, dividing it evenly.

Bake the layers on the lower-third-level rack of the pre-heated oven for 25 to 30 minutes, or until a wooden pick

6 tablespoons (¾ stick) unsalted butter, cut in chunks

½ cup granulated sugar

1 tablespoon cornstarch

¼ cup milk, at room temperature

¼ cup light cream, at room temperature

1 teaspoon pure vanilla extract

One 2-layer 9-inch round cake

inserted in the center of each layer comes out clean and dry and the cake pulls away slightly from the edges of the pan.

Cool the layers in the pans on wire racks for 3 to 5 minutes. Invert the cakes on additional wire racks and peel off the waxed paper if necessary. Let cool completely.

To make the thin and rich frosting, melt the chocolate and butter in a medium-size heavy saucepan. Thoroughly blend together the sugar and cornstarch in a mixing bowl. Combine the milk and light cream and blend into the cornstarch mixture. Off the heat, stir the sugar–milk mixture into the melted butter and chocolate, stirring well. Place the saucepan over moderate heat and bring to a boil, stirring slowly. When the mixture reaches the boil, boil for 1 to 2 minutes, or until moderately thick (the frosting will be thick enough to coat the back of a spoon). Remove from the heat and stir in the vanilla. Let the frosting cool until it reaches a soft spreading consistency, about 15 minutes, depending on the temperature of your kitchen.

Place one of the cake layers on a flat serving dish or cake plate and spread with a little of the frosting. Top with the second cake layer. Spread the remaining frosting over the top and sides of the cake with a flexible palette knife—the frosting will be thin and shiny. (If the frosting is still warm when spread over the cake, it will puddle a bit at the base of the cake; in that case, wait a few minutes for the frosting to firm up, then spread it up against the sides of the cake.) Let the cake sit for about 2 hours to set the frosting.

Serve the cake cut in thick slices.

Coconut Layer Cake

3 cups *sifted* cake flour

2¼ teaspoons baking powder

¼ teaspoon salt

1 cup (2 sticks) unsalted butter, softened at room temperature

1 box (1 pound) confectioners sugar, *sifted*

4 jumbo egg yolks, at room temperature

2 teaspoons pure vanilla extract

1 teaspoon coconut extract

1 cup milk, at room temperature

1⅓ cups (lightly packed) sweetened flaked coconut

4 jumbo egg whites, at room temperature

⅛ teaspoon cream of tartar

This light and high three-layer cake is iced with a billowy white frosting; then the frosting is partially concealed by handfuls of shredded coconut covering the top and sides of the cake. It is a cake reminiscent of the kind you used to find at a diner featuring homemade desserts or a charity bake sale. In my kitchen, you'd see the cake standing tall and proud under a great big Depression-glass cake-keeper. I like to serve the cake with a pot of hot coffee at the close of a Sunday supper, but you can certainly offer it with tall glasses of minted iced tea on an early summer afternoon—an indulgence I heartily recommend.

Lightly butter and flour three 9-inch round cake pans. Line the bottom of each pan with a circle of waxed paper; set aside. Preheat the oven to 350 degrees.

Resift the flour with the baking powder and salt onto a large sheet of waxed paper; set aside. Cream the butter in the large bowl of an electric mixer on moderately high speed for 3 minutes. Reduce the speed to moderate and beat in the confectioners sugar in 4 additions, blending well after each portion is added. Scrape down the sides of the mixing bowl frequently. Continue to cream the butter and sugar on moderately high speed for 3 minutes. Beat in the egg yolks, one at a time, blending well after each one. Blend in the vanilla and coconut extracts. With the mixer on low speed, alternately add the sifted dry ingredients in 3 additions with the milk in 2 additions, beginning and ending

4 jumbo egg whites, at
  room temperature

¾ cup plus 2 table-
  spoons Vanilla-
  Scented Granulated
  Sugar (page 95) or
  plain granulated sugar

Pinch of salt

⅓ cup plus 1½ table-
  spoons light corn
  syrup

1 teaspoon pure vanilla
  extract

FOR FINISHING THE CAKE:

About 2⅔ to 3 cups
  (lightly packed)
  sweetened flaked
  coconut

---

*One 3-layer 9-inch round
cake*

with the dry mixture. By hand, fold in the coconut.

Beat the egg whites until frothy in a clean, dry mixing bowl. Add the cream of tartar and continue beating until firm—but still moist—peaks are formed. Stir 2 large spoonfuls of white into the cake batter to lighten it, then fold in the remaining whites. Divide the batter among the 3 pans, gently leveling the top by shaking each pan from side to side.

Bake the layers on the upper- and lower-third-level racks of the preheated oven for about 30 to 35 minutes, or until a wooden pick inserted in the center of the cakes comes out clean and dry and the layers begin to pull away from the sides of the pan. To ensure even heat distribution, rotate the pans from lower third to upper third and from front to back halfway through the baking time.

Cool the layers in the pans on wire racks for 2 to 3 minutes. Run a thin, flexible palette knife between each layer and the side of the pan. Invert the layers onto cooling racks. Peel off the waxed paper. Let cool completely.

To make the billowy white frosting, combine the egg whites, sugar, salt and corn syrup in the top saucepan of a large double boiler. Fill the bottom with about 1½ inches of water and bring to the barest simmer. (The water should come within ½ inch of the bottom of the top pan but not touch it; adjust the water level accordingly.) Set the top pan over the bottom.

Beat the frosting with a hand-held electric beater on moderate speed for 6 minutes. Add the vanilla, raise the speed to moderately high and continue beating for 1 to 2 minutes longer, or until the frosting is shiny and marshmallow-like. Carefully remove the top saucepan from the water bath, wipe off the bottom and beat for a minute or so to cool the frosting slightly.

Place one cake layer on a flat serving plate and spread with a little frosting. Top with the second layer and spread with a little frosting. Put on the last layer. Peak and swirl the remaining frosting all over the top and sides of the cake. Sprinkle 2⅔ cups coconut heavily over the top and sides of the cake, using an extra ⅓ cup if necessary to cover the whole cake generously.

Serve the cake, cut in slices, on big plates.

COFFEE CAKES

Wendy Wheeler

COFFEE CAKES

—◇◇◇—

Cocoa-Nut Swirl Coffee Cake   48
Coconut–Cinnamon Pan Cake   50
Apple–Raisin Coffee Cake   52
Maple–Pumpkin Coffee Cake   54
Walnut–Sweet Potato Coffee Cake   56
Banana–Coconut Coffee Cake   58
Raspberry Coffee Cake   60
Date Coffee Cake   62
Caramel Upside-Down Sticky Cake   64

A just-out-of-the-oven coffee cake, fragrant and inviting, is what homestyle baking is all about. Moist and full of the flavor of good butter, eggs, spices, nuts and fruit, it is the perfect bit of cake to have around for morning or afternoon snacking. Coffee cake goes down easily with oversized cups of hot coffee, naturally, done right with cream and sugar. Or serve slices of cake with a pitcher of fairly strong iced coffee lightened with cream.

Treat friends or neighbors who stop by your house some afternoon after a round of errands with slices of Apple–Raisin Coffee Cake (page 52), squares of Coconut–Cinnamon Pan Cake (page 50) or fat hunks pulled away from a Caramel Upside-Down Sticky Cake (page 64). To make the coffee and coffee cake hour a more festive event, set out refreshments on a big table spread with a colorful quilt or lacy linen coverlet; arrange napkins, charming plates, silver dessert forks and spoons in a still life along with a variety of cakes, baskets of seasonal fruit and wild flowers.

Cocoa-Nut Swirl Coffee Cake

2½ cups *unsifted* all-purpose flour

2½ teaspoons baking powder

½ teaspoon baking soda

¼ teaspoon salt

¾ teaspoon ground cinnamon

1 cup (2 sticks) unsalted butter, softened at room temperature

1½ cups Vanilla-Scented Granulated Sugar (page 95) or plain granulated sugar

3 extra-large eggs, at room temperature

1 teaspoon pure vanilla extract

1 cup sour cream, at room temperature

FOR THE COCOA-NUT SWIRL MIXTURE:

¼ cup granulated sugar

½ cup finely chopped walnuts

This simple butter cake is fussied up with a blend of sugar, walnuts, cocoa powder and ground cinnamon that meanders through the batter in a curly streak. A close-textured cake, but one that is still quite light, this sweet is a welcome companion to cups of hot coffee or slender glasses of ice-cold lemonade or limeade. Serve thick slices of Cocoa-Nut Swirl Coffee Cake in the morning bread basket, offer thin slices with hot tea on a cool midafternoon, or coat slightly stale slices with a dipping batter of beaten eggs and milk and fry them, French toast-style, and serve at Sunday breakfast.

———❖❖❖———

Lightly butter and flour a plain 9-inch tube pan. Line the bottom of the pan with a circle of waxed paper, trimmed to fit; set aside. Preheat the oven to 325 degrees.

Sift together the flour, baking powder, baking soda, salt and cinnamon onto a large sheet of waxed paper; set aside.

Cream the butter in the large bowl of an electric mixer on moderately high speed for 2 minutes. Add the sugar in 2 additions, beating thoroughly after each portion is added. Beat for 1 minute on high speed. With the mixer on moderately high speed, blend in the eggs, one at a time. Beat in the vanilla. Scrape down the sides of the mixing bowl and beat the mixture for about 30 seconds longer. With the mixer on low speed, alternately add the sifted dry ingredients in 3 additions and the sour cream in 2 additions, beginning and ending with the dry mixture. Scrape down the

3 tablespoons *unsifted* unsweetened cocoa powder

1 teaspoon ground cinnamon

Confectioners sugar for dusting (optional)

One 9-inch tube cake

sides of the mixing bowl frequently with a rubber spatula to keep the batter even-textured.

For the cocoa-nut swirl, combine the sugar, walnuts, cocoa and cinnamon in a small bowl.

Pour and scrape half the batter into the prepared baking pan. Sprinkle the cocoa-nut swirl mixture evenly over the batter. Pour the rest of the batter on top.

Bake the cake on the lower-third-level rack of the pre-heated oven for about 50 minutes to 1 hour, or until a wooden pick inserted in the center of the cake comes out clean and dry and the cake pulls away slightly from the edges of the pan.

Let cool in the pan on a wire rack for 4 to 5 minutes. Invert onto a second cooling rack, then invert again to cool right side up. Dust the top of the cake with a little sifted confectioners sugar, if you like.

Serve the cake cut in medium thick slices.

Coconut–Cinnamon Pan Cake

1½ cups *unsifted* all-purpose flour

2 teaspoons baking powder

¼ teaspoon salt

1 teaspoon ground cinnamon

½ teaspoon freshly grated nutmeg

¼ teaspoon ground allspice

½ cup (1 stick) unsalted butter, softened at room temperature

½ cup granulated sugar

½ cup (firmly packed) light brown sugar

1 extra-large egg, at room temperature

2 extra-large egg yolks, at room temperature

½ cup milk, at room temperature, blended with 2 teaspoons pure vanilla extract

Underneath all of the spices and the coconut–butter crumble of this recipe is a very simple formula for a butter cake made in a square pan. I was first taught how to make it in a home economics class at the age of eight. Years later, I made a marvelous little coffee cake out of the main ingredients, and since then, I bake the cake often to serve with tea or at brunch. It is delicious cut in squares and served with whipped cream, a bowl of berries and a pot of herbal tea for a casual midafternoon break. Cake left over to the next day can be warmed and served at breakfast. Or layer a bowl with cubes of cake, custard and sweetened berries to make a splendid summer pudding.

———◆◆◆———

Lightly butter and flour a 10-inch square cake pan and line the bottom with waxed paper; set aside. Preheat the oven to 350 degrees.

Sift together the flour, baking powder, salt, cinnamon, nutmeg and allspice onto a large sheet of waxed paper.

Cream the butter in the large bowl of an electric mixer on moderately high speed for 2 to 3 minutes. Beat in the granulated sugar; continue beating for 2 minutes. Add the brown sugar and beat for 1 minute longer. Beat in the egg and egg yolks and blend well. With the mixer on low speed, alternately add the sifted flour mixture in 2 additions with the milk in 1 addition, beginning and ending with flour. Spoon the batter into the prepared pan; spread evenly.

2½ tablespoons unsalted
  butter, cut in small
  bits, cold

¼ cup (firmly packed)
  light brown sugar

1 tablespoon *unsifted* all-
  purpose flour

¾ cup sweetened
  shredded coconut

¼ cup chopped walnuts

_____

One 10-inch square cake

For the coconut–butter crumble, place the butter, brown sugar, flour, coconut and walnuts in a bowl. Mix all of the ingredients together with your fingertips until it looks like a rough streusel, making sure that the butter is broken down into small bits. Sprinkle the crumble evenly over the top of the cake batter.

Bake the cake on the lower-third-level rack of the pre-heated oven for about 40 minutes, or until a wooden pick inserted into the center of the cake comes out clean and dry and the cake pulls slightly away from the sides of the pan.

Let cool in the pan on a wire rack for 5 to 10 minutes. Carefully invert the cake onto a second cooling rack and peel away the waxed paper; invert again to cool right side up.

Serve the cake warm or at room temperature, cut in squares.

Apple–Raisin Coffee Cake

1¾ cups *unsifted* all-purpose flour

1 teaspoon baking powder

½ teaspoon baking soda

¼ teaspoon salt

1 teaspoon ground cinnamon

¼ teaspoon freshly grated nutmeg

¼ teaspoon ground allspice

¼ cup dark seedless raisins

½ cup (1 stick) unsalted butter, softened at room temperature

¾ cup granulated sugar

2 extra-large eggs, at room temperature

2 teaspoons pure vanilla extract

3 tablespoons light cream

1 cup (tightly packed) peeled, cored and

Thin slices cut from this firm-textured, moderately sweet loaf are appealing served at breakfast with coffee or tea. The cake can also be paired with hot mulled cider for a warming snack. Dark seedless raisins, incorporated in the batter along with the shreds of apple, add a pleasant sweetness to each slice. If your raisins are not as moist as they should be, plump them up in hot apple juice or cider. Apple–Raisin Coffee Cake keeps nicely for a week stored in an airtight tin or cake-keeper.

————◈◈◈————

Lightly butter and flour a 10 x 3¾ x 3 inch loaf pan; set aside. Preheat the oven to 350 degrees.

Sift together the flour, baking powder, baking soda, salt, cinnamon, nutmeg and allspice onto a large sheet of waxed paper. Place the raisins in a small bowl and toss with 1 teaspoon of the sifted mixture.

Cream the butter in the large bowl of an electric mixer on moderately high speed for 2 to 3 minutes. Add the sugar in 2 additions, beating well for 1 to 2 minutes after each portion is added. Beat in the eggs, one at a time, blending well after each one. Scrape down the sides of the bowl with a rubber spatula and beat again for a few seconds. Blend in the vanilla and cream. With the mixer on low speed, add the sifted flour mixture, beating just until the particles of flour have been absorbed. By hand, stir in the apple and raisins. Spoon the batter into the prepared pan.

shredded tart apple,
such as Granny Smith

Confectioners sugar for
dusting (optional)

---

*One 10 x 3¾ x 3-inch loaf
cake*

Bake the cake on the lower-third-level rack of the pre-heated oven for about 50 minutes, or until a wooden pick inserted into the center of the cake comes out clean and dry.

Let cool in the pan on a wire rack for 4 to 5 minutes. Invert onto a second cooling rack, then invert again to cool right side up. Dust the cooled loaf with sifted confectioners sugar, if you like.

Serve the cake cut in medium thick slices.

Maple–Pumpkin Coffee Cake

2 cups *unsifted* all-
  purpose flour

2 teaspoons baking
  powder

¼ teaspoon baking soda

¼ teaspoon salt

1 teaspoon ground
  cinnamon

¼ teaspoon freshly
  grated nutmeg

¼ teaspoon ground
  allspice

¼ teaspoon ground
  ginger

⅛ teaspoon ground
  cloves

⅓ cup chopped pecans

¼ cup dark seedless
  raisins

4 tablespoons (½ stick)
  unsalted butter,
  melted and cooled

½ cup (firmly packed)
  light brown sugar

¼ cup granulated sugar

2 extra-large eggs, at
  room temperature

This rust-colored loaf cake has a soft texture and fine, delicate crumb. Slices seem made for pairing with hot, strong coffee and a warm fruit compote simmered with whole spices. It is also a good morning cake to serve with butter and jam. I love this cake because it is not too sweet. Sometimes, at Thanksgiving for instance, I sneak triangles of this cake into a bread basket already loaded with corn muffins and biscuits—and watch them disappear.

———❖❖❖———

Lightly butter and flour a 10 x 3¾ x 3-inch loaf pan; set aside. Preheat the oven to 350 degrees.

Sift together the flour, baking powder, baking soda, salt, cinnamon, nutmeg, allspice, ginger and cloves onto a large sheet of waxed paper. Place the pecans and raisins in a small bowl and toss with 2 teaspoons of the sifted mixture.

Stir together the melted butter, brown sugar and granulated sugar in a large mixing bowl, using a wooden spoon. Beat in the eggs and vanilla. Blend in the maple syrup-milk mixture and the pumpkin puree. Add the sifted dry ingredients and stir with a wooden spoon. Fold in the floured pecans and raisins. Spoon the batter into the prepared pan.

Bake the cake on the lower-third-level rack of the preheated oven for about 45 minutes, or until the cake is well-risen and plump and a wooden pick inserted into the center of the cake comes out clean and dry.

Let cool in the pan on a wire rack for 5 minutes. Invert onto a second cooling rack, then invert again to cool right

2 teaspoons pure vanilla extract

2 tablespoons pure maple syrup blended with 2 tablespoons milk

1 cup unsweetened pumpkin puree, fresh (recipe follows) or canned

Confectioners sugar for dusting (optional)

One 10 x 3¾ x 3-inch loaf cake

side up. Dust the top of the cooled cake with sifted confectioners sugar, if you like.

Serve the cake cut in medium thick slices.

Homemade Pumpkin Puree

Cut a small pumpkin (4 to 5 pounds) in half, using a large knife or cleaver. Scoop out the pumpkin seeds with a spoon and discard them or clean off the filaments and roast the seeds in the oven (they are delicious to snack on). Cut the pumpkin flesh into very large chunks, roughly 3 inches square. Place the chunks in a steamer basket and steam over moderately high heat until the flesh has softened completely, about 15 minutes. Let cool completely. Scrape the flesh from the skin, then puree the flesh with a large pinch of salt in the workbowl of a food processor fitted with the steel knife or with a food mill or potato ricer. Spoon 1-cup quantities of the puree into sturdy storage containers. Press a piece of plastic wrap directly over the top, then seal with the lid. The puree will keep in the refrigerator for up to 1 week or in the freezer for up to 6 months.

Walnut–Sweet Potato Coffee Cake

A butter-rich cinnamon, walnut and sugar topping caps off this modestly sweetened but amply spiced coffee cake. Serve it in thin slices at teatime, with dollops of cinnamon-flavored whipped cream.

———◆◆◆———

2 cups *unsifted* all-purpose flour

2 teaspoons baking powder

¼ teaspoon baking soda

½ teaspoon salt

1 teaspoon ground cinnamon

½ teaspoon freshly grated nutmeg

¼ teaspoon ground allspice

¼ teaspoon ground ginger

½ cup chopped walnuts

4 tablespoons (½ stick) unsalted butter, melted and cooled

⅓ cup (firmly packed) light brown sugar

⅓ cup granulated sugar

2 extra-large eggs, at room temperature

2 tablespoons milk, at room temperature

Lightly butter and flour a 10 x 3¾ x 3-inch loaf pan; set aside. Preheat the oven to 350 degrees.

Sift together the flour, baking powder, baking soda, salt, cinnamon, nutmeg, allspice and ginger onto a large sheet of waxed paper. Place the walnuts in a small bowl and toss with 1 teaspoon of the sifted mixture.

Stir together the melted butter, brown sugar and granulated sugar in a large mixing bowl, using a wooden spoon or flat paddle. Beat in the eggs, one at a time, blending well after each one. Beat in the milk, cream, vanilla, orange rind and pureed sweet potatoes. Add the sifted flour mixture and stir. Fold in the floured walnuts. Spoon the batter into the prepared pan.

For the topping, put the butter cubes, walnuts, sugar and cinnamon in a small mixing bowl. Crumble the mixture together with your fingertips until the butter is broken down into small bits. Sprinkle the topping evenly over the top of the cake.

Bake the cake on the lower-third-level rack of the preheated oven for about 45 minutes, or until a wooden pick inserted into the center of the cake comes out clean and dry and the cake pulls slightly away from the edges of the pan.

2 tablespoons light
  cream, at room
  temperature

1 teaspoon pure vanilla
  extract

2 teaspoons finely grated
  orange rind

1 cup steamed and
  pureed sweet potatoes,
  at room temperature

FOR THE CINNAMON—
WALNUT TOPPING:

2 tablespoons unsalted
  butter, cut in small
  cubes, cold

4 tablespoons chopped
  walnuts

3 tablespoons granulated
  sugar

1 teaspoon ground
  cinnamon

---

*One 10 x 3¾ x 3-inch loaf
cake*

Let cool in the pan on a wire rack for 5 minutes. Invert onto a second cooling rack, then invert again to cool right side up.

Serve the cake cut in medium thick slices.

Banana– Coconut Coffee Cake

2 cups *unsifted* all-
 purpose flour

1 teaspoon baking
 powder

¼ teaspoon baking soda

¼ teaspoon salt

½ teaspoon ground
 cinnamon

½ teaspoon freshly
 grated nutmeg

¼ teaspoon ground
 allspice

¼ cup chopped unsalted
 pecans

½ cup (1 stick) unsalted
 butter, softened at
 room temperature

¾ cup (firmly packed)
 light brown sugar

1 extra-large egg, at
 room temperature

2 extra-large egg yolks,
 at room temperature

1 teaspoon pure vanilla
 extract

This loaf of many flavors is graced with chopped pecans, mashed bananas and flaked coconut. Right before the cake is put into the oven to bake, I sprinkle the top with lightly toasted coconut. Banana–Coconut Coffee Cake makes a mighty fine munching cake, a sweet breakfast bread or a lush tea cake when served with poached fresh fruit.

This is an old, treasured recipe of mine, based on my grandmother's banana–coconut bread. I add a little more butter than she did, and use brown sugar instead of granu-lated sugar; I also add ground cinnamon with the nutmeg and allspice. Then I like to top the loaf with lightly toasted coconut just before baking. Some twenty years ago, I baked 50 loaves of Banana–Coconut Coffee Cake for a country fair, and not a crumb was left. I was inundated with requests for the recipe—so here it is!

————— ✦✦✦ —————

Lightly butter and flour a 9 x 5 x 3-inch loaf pan; set aside. Preheat the oven to 350 degrees.

Sift together the flour, baking powder, baking soda, salt, cinnamon, nutmeg and allspice onto a large sheet of waxed paper. Place the chopped pecans in a small bowl and toss with ½ teaspoon of the sifted flour mixture.

Cream the butter in the large bowl of an electric mixer on moderately high speed for 2 to 3 minutes. Add the brown sugar and continue beating for 1 to 2 minutes. Beat in the egg and egg yolks. Beat in the vanilla. Blend in the mashed bananas. With the mixer on low speed, add the sifted flour

1½ cups mashed ripe
    bananas (2 bananas)

½ cup sweetened flaked
    coconut

FOR FINISHING THE CAKE:

¼ cup sweetened flaked
    coconut, lightly
    toasted (see Note)

One 9 x 5 x 3-inch loaf cake

mixture in 2 additions, beating just until the particles of flour have been absorbed. By hand, stir in the pecans and shredded coconut. Spoon the batter into the prepared pan.

Sprinkle the top of the batter with the toasted coconut.

Bake the cake on the lower-third-level rack of the preheated oven for 50 to 55 minutes, or until well risen and a wooden pick inserted into the center of the cake comes out clean and dry. The cake will pull away slightly from the edges of the pan when done.

Let cool in the pan on a wire rack for 5 minutes. Invert onto a second cooling rack, then invert again to cool right side up.

Serve the cake cut in medium thick slices.

Note: To toast the coconut, preheat the oven to 350 degrees. Spread out the coconut on a small baking pan and place in the preheated oven. After about 4 to 5 minutes, the coconut should turn golden and fragrant. Remove from the oven and cool completely before using. Alternately, the coconut can be toasted under the broiler: Spread the coconut on a cookie sheet and place 4 inches from the broiler. After 1 minute, the coconut should be toasted. Watch carefully to avoid burning.

Raspberry Coffee Cake

2 cups *unsifted* cake flour

1 teaspoon baking powder

¾ teaspoon baking soda

¼ teaspoon salt

¼ teaspoon ground cinnamon

¼ teaspoon ground nutmeg

Pinch of ground allspice

1¼ cups fresh red raspberries, picked over

½ cup (1 stick) unsalted butter, softened at room temperature

½ cup plus 1 tablespoon Vanilla-Scented Granulated Sugar (page 95) or plain granulated sugar

1 extra-large egg, at room temperature

2 extra-large egg yolks, at room temperature

¼ cup plain yogurt, at room temperature,

This is a soft, fresh-tasing coffee cake dressed up with red raspberries and energized by a trio of spices. Just before baking, the loaf is topped with a hazy wash of chopped walnuts, sugar, cinnamon and butter. Serve warm slabs of this cake with English breakfast tea or tall, frosty glasses of iced lemon tea.

———◆◆◆———

Lightly butter and flour a 9 x 5 x 3-inch loaf pan; set aside. Preheat the oven to 350 degrees.

Resift the flour with the baking powder, baking soda, salt, cinnamon, nutmeg and allspice onto a large sheet of waxed paper. Place the raspberries in a bowl and carefully toss with 1 tablespoon of the sifted mixture.

Cream the butter in the large bowl of an electric mixer on moderately high speed for 2 minutes. Add the sugar and continue beating for 2 minutes longer. Beat in the egg and egg yolks and blend well. Scrape down the sides of the bowl with a rubber spatula, then beat for a moment or two longer. With the mixer on low speed, alternately add the sifted flour mixture in 2 additions and the yogurt–vanilla blend in 1 addition, beginning and ending with flour. By hand, fold in the floured raspberries. Spoon the batter into the prepared loaf pan.

For the topping, place the cold butter cubes, walnuts, sugar and cinnamon in a mixing bowl. Crumble the mixture together with your fingertips until the butter is reduced to smaller bits. Sprinkle batter evenly with the topping.

blended with
2 teaspoons pure
vanilla extract

FOR THE WALNUT TOPPING:

1 tablespoon unsalted
  butter, cut in small
  cubes, cold
2½ tablespoons chopped
  walnuts
2 tablespoons granulated
  sugar
½ teaspoon ground
  cinnamon

One 9 x 5 x 3-inch loaf cake

Bake the cake on the lower-third-level rack of the pre-heated oven for about 45 minutes, or until a wooden pick inserted into the center of the cake comes out without any clinging particles of cake batter (the pick will be tinted pink if you bump into a raspberry).

Let cool in the pan on a wire rack for 4 to 5 minutes. Carefully invert onto a second cooling rack, then invert again to cool right side up.

Serve the cake cut in medium thick slices.

Date Coffee Cake

1¼ cups milk

1¾ cups coarsely chopped pitted dates

2½ cups *unsifted* all-purpose flour

1¾ teaspoons baking soda

¼ teaspoon salt

¾ teaspoon ground cinnamon

¼ teaspoon freshly grated nutmeg

¼ teaspoon ground allspice

¾ cups chopped walnuts

2 jumbo egg yolks, at room temperature

3 tablespoons unsalted butter, melted and cooled

2 teaspoons pure vanilla extract

¾ cup granulated sugar

½ cup (firmly packed) light brown sugar

One 9 x 5 x 3-inch loaf cake

A long-keeping, firm-textured coffee cake such as this is a fine thing to have in the cake tin. It combines several textures and tastes: chewy dates and crunchy walnuts, the caramel flavor of brown sugar and a whiff of cinnamon and nutmeg. The dates—sticky, rich and sweet—keep this cake moist and fresh-tasting for some time; the cake stores perfectly at room temperature (I keep the loaf in my bread box). Slices of Date Coffee Cake can keep company with large cups of spiced cider, hot coffee or orange tea.

This recipe is from my Aunt Mamie, who made this loaf every weekend. I have made a few small changes in the original recipe, such as adding a little more brown sugar and cinnamon to the batter. Freshly ground nutmeg, of which she added only a pinch, has been upgraded to ¼ teaspoon.

———❖❖❖———

Lightly butter and flour a 9 x 5 x 3-inch loaf pan; set aside. Preheat the oven to 350 degrees.

Heat the milk in a saucepan until tepid. Place the dates in a large bowl, pour the milk over them and let stand for 20 minutes. Sift together the flour, baking soda, salt, cinnamon, nutmeg and allspice onto a large sheet of waxed paper. Place the walnuts in a small bowl and toss with 1 teaspoon of the sifted flour mixture.

Beat together the egg yolks, melted butter, vanilla and granulated sugar in a large mixing bowl, using a wooden spoon or paddle. Beat in the brown sugar. Stir in the milk–

date mixture. Stir in the sifted flour mixture in 2 additions, stirring just until the particles of flour have been absorbed before adding the next batch of flour. Fold in the walnuts. Spoon the batter into the prepared pan.

Bake the cake on the lower-third-level rack of the preheated oven for 50 minutes to 1 hour, or until a wooden pick inserted into the center of the loaf comes out clean and dry. The cake will pull away slightly from the sides of the pan when done.

Let the cake cool in the pan on a wire rack for 4 to 5 minutes. Invert onto a second cooling rack, then invert again to cool right side up.

Serve the cake cut in moderately thin slices.

Caramel Upside-Down Sticky Cake

FOR THE DOUGH:

1 package (1 scant tablespoon) active dry yeast

¼ cup granulated sugar

1 teaspoon salt

3¼ cups *unsifted* all-purpose flour, plus extra flour as necessary

⅓ cup water

⅓ cup light cream

½ cup (1 stick) unsalted butter, cut into chunks

2 extra-large egg yolks, at room temperature

1 teaspoon pure vanilla extract

¼ teaspoon freshly ground nutmeg

FOR THE STICKY MIXTURE:

2 tablespoons unsalted butter

¼ cup light corn syrup

Sticky cake is a light, yeasty cake. Puffy dough is rolled into a large square, slathered with softened butter and sprinkled with spiced sugar, then rolled into a fat sausage and cut in thick pieces. These soft packages of dough are then laid in a square pan filled with heavy caramel syrup. The syrup is sticky and buttery, and you can scatter such things as chopped pecans, walnuts or shredded coconut on it before setting in the spirals of dough. The dough for this cake is a pleasure to work with; it's silky to the touch, rolls out magnificently and can be fashioned into any number of shapes, even free-standing tea rings or twists. A warm piece of sticky cake makes as fine a Sunday morning breakfast treat as anyone could imagine.

For the dough, thoroughly combine the yeast, sugar, salt and 2 cups of flour in a large mixing bowl. Put water, cream and butter into a small saucepan and heat until the liquid reaches a temperature of 125 degrees (hot to the touch). Remove from the heat and pour over the flour mixture. Add the egg yolks, and vanilla and nutmeg. Stir everything together with a wooden spoon or paddle. With your hands, work in the remaining flour, a little at a time, to form a soft dough. Turn the dough onto a lightly floured work surface and knead until it is supple and satiny, about 7 to 8 minutes. Place the dough in a buttered bowl, turning several times to coat it lightly in butter. Cover loosely with a sheet of plastic wrap or a tea towel and let rise in a draft-free spot until doubled in bulk, about 1½ to 2 hours.

¼ cup (firmly packed) light brown sugar

3 tablespoons granulated sugar

FOR THE CINNAMON–SUGAR FILLING:

3 tablespoons unsalted butter, softened at room temperature

½ cup granulated sugar

1 tablespoon (firmly packed) light brown sugar

1 tablespoon ground cinnamon

¼ teaspoon freshly grated nutmeg

One 10-inch square pull-apart cake

While the dough is rising, make the sticky mixture. Spray a 10-inch square baking pan with vegetable-oil cooking spray; set aside. Place the butter, corn syrup, brown sugar and granulated sugar in a small, heavy saucepan. Cover the pan and set over low heat. Cook until every granule of sugar has dissolved, about 10 minutes. Uncover the pot, raise the heat to moderately high and boil for 1½ to 2 minutes, or until lightly thickened. Pour into the prepared baking pan.

Punch down the risen dough in the bowl. Turn it out onto a lightly floured work surface and let it rest for 5 minutes. Using a lightly floured rolling pin, roll out the dough into a rough square, about 13 x 13 inches. Spread the softened butter over the surface of the dough. Combine the granulated sugar, brown sugar, cinnamon and nutmeg in a small bowl; sprinkle over the butter. Roll up the dough tightly, like a jelly roll. Cut into 9 equal pieces with a sharp knife. Arrange the pieces, cut side up, 3 to a row, in the caramel-lined baking pan. Cover loosely and let rise in a draft-free spot until doubled in bulk, about 1½ to 2 hours. The individual rounds of dough will rise together to form a solid cake.

About 20 minutes before the end of the rising time, preheat the oven to 375 degrees. Bake the cake on the lower-third-level rack of the preheated oven for about 30 minutes, or until golden on top and baked through (a wooden pick inserted into one section of the cake should come out clean).

Let stand in the pan on a cooling rack for 1 minute, then invert the cake onto a serving plate.

Serve the cake warm or at room temperature, sticky side up; let everyone pull apart a portion.

TRAVELING
CAKES

Wendy Wheeler

TRAVELING CAKES

---✦✦✦---

Blueberry—Walnut—Brown Sugar Buckle   70
Chocolate Pan Cake with Chocolate Fudge Frosting   72
Pecan Carrot Cake with Raisins   74
Fudgy Chocolate—Walnut Cake   76

*F*or leisurely bring-a-dish suppers, when guests are encouraged to contribute part of the meal, a delicious cake, made entirely in advance, is just the thing. I call these portable goodies traveling cakes for their ability to withstand bumpy road trips and still look fresh. They are baked in simple square, rectangular or round baking pans and are left in the pan until cut at serving time. Oftentimes at flea markets and tag sales or antique shows featuring Americana artifacts, you'll come across old baking tins with snap-on lids for traveling; the domed lid, used to cover an iced or uniced cake, protects it during transportation. Traveling cakes are easy to make, they appeal to children and grown-ups alike, and they use ingredients that even casual bakers have on hand. Their rough-and-ready nature makes it possible to transport them easily.

Other cakes that are well-suited to packing in a picnic hamper or slicing and tucking into a lunch box are Best Vanilla Pound Cake (page 94), Lemon–Poppy Seed Pound Cake (page 98), Chocolate Pound Cake (page 108), Bourbon Pound Cake (page 100), Spice Pound Cake (page 102), Cream Pound Cake (page 106), Spicy Apple Cake (page 116), Blueberry Gingerbread (page 122), Ginger Cakes (page 130), Blueberry Cakes (page 132), Cream Cheese–Chocolate Chip Cakes (page 134), Vanilla Cakes (page 136), Coconut–Cinnamon Pan Cake (page 50), Apple–Raisin Coffee Cake (page 52), Maple–Pumpkin Coffee Cake (page 54), Banana–Coconut Coffee Cake (page 58), Date Coffee Cake (page 62) and Plum Cake (page 114).

Blueberry–Walnut–Brown Sugar Buckle

1¾ cups *unsifted* all-purpose flour

3 teaspoons baking powder

½ teaspoon salt

½ teaspoon ground cinnamon

¼ teaspoon freshly grated nutmeg

¼ teaspoon ground allspice

⅔ cup blueberries, picked over

½ cup (1 stick) unsalted butter, softened at room temperature

¼ cup (firmly packed) light brown sugar

¼ cup granulated sugar

2 extra-large eggs, at room temperature

2 teaspoons pure vanilla extract

1 cup milk, at room temperature

This cake tastes of summer: plump blueberries, sweet and fruity, dot a buttery square cake. The batter contains a fair measure of brown sugar, which enhances the taste of blueberries, and a restrained trio of spices. The buckle is best eaten very fresh and still warm, while the sandy topping is still soft. Homemade lemonade is a natural partner.

————◆◆◆————

Lightly butter and flour an 8-inch square baking pan. Line the bottom of the pan with a square of waxed paper; set aside. Preheat the oven to 350 degrees.

Sift together the flour, baking powder, salt, cinnamon, nutmeg and allspice onto a large sheet of waxed paper. Place the blueberries in a bowl and toss with 1 tablespoon of the sifted mixture.

Cream the butter in the large bowl of an electric mixer on moderately high speed for 2 minutes. Add the brown sugar and granulated sugar; beat for 2 minutes. Beat in the eggs, one at a time, blending well after each one. Scrape down the sides of the bowl with a rubber spatula and beat again for a few moments longer. Blend in the vanilla. With the mixer on low speed, alternately add the sifted dry ingredients in 3 additions and the milk in 2 additions, beginning and ending with the dry mixture. Fold in the blueberries. Spoon the batter into the prepared pan.

To make the crumble, put the butter, walnuts, sugar and cinnamon in a mixing bowl. Crumble everything together with your fingertips until the butter is reduced to small bits.

FOR THE WALNUT—BROWN SUGAR CRUMBLE TOPPING:

2 tablespoons unsalted butter, cut in cubes, cold

¼ cup chopped walnuts

3 tablespoons (firmly packed) light brown sugar

1 teaspoon ground cinnamon

Confectioners sugar for dusting (optional)

One 8-inch square cake

Sprinkle the crumble evenly over the top of the batter.

Bake the cake on the lower-third-level rack of the preheated oven for 45 to 50 minutes, or until a wooden pick inserted in the center comes out without any particles of cake clinging to it. The cake will shrink slightly from the sides of the pan when done.

Let cool in the pan on a wire rack. Transport the cake as is or invert it onto a second cooling rack, peel away the waxed paper and invert again onto a serving plate. Dust the top of the cake with a little sifted confectioners sugar, if you like.

Serve the cake cut in squares.

Chocolate Pan Cake with Chocolate Fudge Frosting

The formula for this cake is really a conspiracy of chocolate. The chocolate cake is light and creamy, and while it is still oven-hot, it is completely covered over with a dense, rich fudge frosting flecked with plenty of chopped pecans. Children love big squares of this cake with a glass of cold milk. The recipe comes from my friend and good cook Alice Romejko, who likes to serve the cake at buffet suppers.

FOR THE CAKE:

1 cup (2 sticks) unsalted butter, cut in rough chunks

4 tablespoons *unsifted* unsweetened cocoa powder

1 cup water

2 cups granulated sugar

2 cups *unsifted* cake flour

1 teaspoon salt

½ cup buttermilk, at room temperature, blended with 1 teaspoon baking soda

2 extra-large eggs, at room temperature

1½ teaspoons pure vanilla extract

Lightly butter and flour a 9 x 13 x 2-inch cake pan; set aside. Preheat the oven to 400 degrees.

For the cake, place the butter, cocoa and water in a large saucepan, set over moderately high heat and bring to a boil. Remove from the heat. Sift together the sugar, flour and salt into the large bowl of an electric mixer. Whisk together the buttermilk, eggs and vanilla in a mixing bowl. Pour the hot butter–cocoa–water mixture over the sifted dry mixture and beat on moderate speed until thoroughly blended. Add the whisked egg mixture and continue beating on low speed until the batter is a uniform color, about 1½ minutes. Pour and scrape the batter into the prepared pan.

Bake the cake on the lower-third-level rack of the preheated oven for 20 to 22 minutes, or until a wooden pick inserted into the center of the cake comes out clean and dry and the cake shrinks away slightly from the edges of the pan.

About 10 minutes before the cake is done, make the fudge frosting. Place the butter, chocolate, milk and cream

FOR THE CHOCOLATE FUDGE FROSTING:

½ cup (1 stick) unsalted butter, cut in chunks

2 ounces (2 squares) unsweetened chocolate, chopped

5 tablespoons milk, at room temperature

1 tablespoon light cream, at room temperature

1 box (1-pound) confectioners sugar, *sifted*

1 teaspoon pure vanilla extract

Pinch of salt

1 cup chopped pecans

One 9 x 13-inch cake

in a large saucepan, set over low heat and cook, stirring occasionally, until the chocolate has melted down completely. Remove from the heat and beat in the sugar by cupfuls with the vanilla and salt. Blend in the pecans.

As soon as the cake is done, remove it from the oven to a wire cooling rack. Immediately spread the frosting evenly over the top with a flexible palette knife. Let the cake cool in the pan.

For serving, cut the cake in squares directly from the cake pan.

Note: I use 1 teaspoon more vanilla in the cake batter than Alice's recipe calls for and a mixture of milk and light cream in the frosting. For the frosting, you can use all milk (6 tablespoons), if you like.

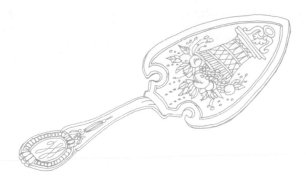

Pecan Carrot Cake with Raisins

1½ cups plus 2 table-
  spoons *unsifted* cake
  flour

1½ teaspoons baking
  powder

1 teaspoon baking soda

¼ teaspoon salt

1½ teaspoons ground
  cinnamon

1 teaspoon freshly
  grated nutmeg

½ teaspoon ground
  allspice

¼ teaspoon ground
  cloves

¾ cup chopped pecans

¾ cup dark seedless
  raisins

½ cup (1 stick) unsalted
  butter, melted and
  cooled

½ cup (firmly packed)
  light brown sugar

½ cup granulated sugar

Laced with pecans and raisins, this cake is moist and flavor-ful; the thin carrot shreds virtually melt down in the batter as the cake bakes, creating a crumb that is soft and golden. Cinnamon is the top note of spices, supported by nutmeg, allspice and cloves. The top of the cake is covered with a thick mantle of simple vanilla cream frosting. Lightly toasted chopped pecans can be sprinkled over the icing once it has set up, if you like.

Lightly butter and flour a 9-inch round springform pan; set aside. Preheat the oven to 350 degrees.

Sift together the flour, baking powder, baking soda, salt, cinnamon, nutmeg, allspice and cloves into a large mixing bowl. Place the pecans and raisins in a bowl and toss with 1 tablespoon of the sifted mixture.

Whisk together the butter, brown sugar, granulated sugar, egg, egg yolks, vanilla, milk and cream in a medium-size bowl. Make a large well in the center of the dry ingredients, pour in the whisked mixture and stir with a wooden spoon until a smooth batter is formed. Fold in the walnuts, raisins and shredded carrots. Spoon the batter into the pre-pared pan.

Bake the cake on the lower-third-level rack of the pre-heated oven for about 45 minutes, or until a wooden pick inserted in the center of the cake comes out clean and dry and the cake pulls away slightly from edges of the pan.

Let the cake cool in the pan on a wire rack.

1 extra-large egg, at
room temperature

2 extra-large egg yolks,
at room temperature

2 teaspoons pure vanilla
extract

¾ cup milk, at room
temperature

¼ cup light cream, at
room temperature

1½ cups shredded
carrots (about 3
carrots)

FOR THE VANILLA CREAM
FROSTING:

2 tablespoons unsalted
butter, softened at
room temperature

2 tablespoons heavy
cream, at room
temperature

½ teaspoon pure vanilla
extract

About 1½ cups
confectioners sugar,
sifted, or more as
needed

One 9-inch round cake

For the vanilla cream frosting, place the butter, heavy
cream, vanilla and ¾ cup of the confectioners sugar in a
small bowl. Beat with a hand-held mixer on moderate speed
for 2 to 3 minutes. Add the remaining ¾ cup of confectioners sugar, several tablespoons at a time, beating well
after each addition, to make a firm, but spreadable frosting.
Add up to ¼ cup more confectioners sugar, if needed to
make the frosting thick and spreadable.

Remove the hinged ring from the cake pan. Swirl the
frosting over the top of the cooled cake. To transport the
cake, you can replace the ring once the icing has firmed up.

Serve the cake cut in large wedges.

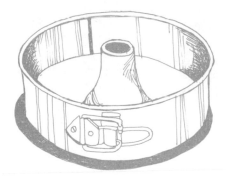

Fudgy Chocolate– Walnut Cake

4 ounces (4 squares) unsweetened chocolate, chopped

½ cup (1 stick) unsalted butter, cut in chunks

⅔ cup *unsifted* cake flour

¼ teaspoon baking powder

½ teaspoon salt

1 jumbo egg, at room temperature

2 jumbo egg yolks, at room temperature

2 teaspoons pure vanilla extract

1 teaspoon chocolate extract

1 cup plus 3 tablespoons Vanilla-Scented Granulated Sugar (page 95)

¾ cup chopped walnuts

Confectioners sugar for dusting (optional)

One 8-inch round cake

This thin chocolate cake has been in my cake file for many cake-baking years. I inherited the recipe from my grandmother; she frequently substituted black walnuts for the more subtle English variety. I make this cake often when what I want is a fudgy sweet that's quick to put together. I have served wedges of the cake with many different accompaniments—vanilla custard sauce, red raspberries and whipped cream, vanilla ice cream with hot fudge sauce. Just for fun, try folding in a cup of chopped thin mints (the candy with a mint layer sandwiched between two chocolate layers) or the same amount of diced caramels with the walnuts.

———❖❖❖———

Lightly butter and flour an 8-inch round cake pan. Line the pan with a round of waxed paper; set aside. Preheat the oven to 350 degrees.

Place the chopped chocolate and butter chunks in a small saucepan and set over low heat. Cook, stirring occasionally, until the chocolate and butter have melted down completely. Set aside to cool.

Stir together the flour, baking powder and salt in a small bowl. Beat the egg and egg yolks with a whisk for 1 minute in a large mixing bowl. Blend in the vanilla and chocolate extracts. Blend in the sugar, beating for 1 minute or until just combined. Stir in the cooled chocolate mixture. Stir in the flour, mixing just until the particles of flour have been absorbed. Fold in ½ cup of the walnuts. Spoon the batter into the prepared pan. Spread the batter evenly in the pan. Sprinkle the remaining ¼ cup of walnuts evenly over the top.

Bake the cake on the lower-third-level rack of the preheated oven for 40 to 45 minutes, until just set; a wooden pick inserted 1 inch from the center will come out damp.

Let cool in the pan on a wire rack until the cake reaches room temperature. Carefully run a thin, flexible palette knife between the edges of the cake and the pan, then invert onto a second cooling rack. Peel away the round of waxed paper. Invert again onto a decorative plate, nut side up. Dust the top of the cake with sifted confectioners sugar, if you like.

Serve the cake cut in wedges.

TEATIME UPSIDE-DOWN CAKES

Wendy Wheeler

TEATIME UPSIDE-DOWN CAKES

————◆◆◆————

Peach Upside-Down Cake 82
Spiced Nectarine Upside-Down Cake 84
Apple–Ginger Upside-Down Cake 86

*O*ne of the most enchanting teatimes I can remember was at a cottage hidden in the Virginia countryside. I arrived one late-summer after-noon, just as the hostess was setting up tea and cakes in the garden. It was a rambling kind of garden, full of fruit trees, shade trees, ornamental plantings and herbs. Tea was offered in pretty floral-patterned china cups, and we tasted a variety of upside-down cakes made from ripe fruit picked just steps away from the kitchen door.

A slice of fresh fruit cake and a cup of hot tea or a tall glass of iced tea can be a marvelous summertime refreshment. And with recipes at hand for Peach Upside-Down Cake (page 82), Spiced Nectarine Upside-Down Cake (page 84), and Apple–Ginger Upside-Down Cake (page 86), you can bring a little bit of the country into your home. Remember that fresh fruit cakes are best eaten warm. That's when the full, sprightly flavor of the fruit comes through best. Fruited upside-down cakes, cut into neat wedges, taste good with dollops of lightly sweetened whipped cream spooned on top.

Peach Upside-Down Cake

FOR PREPARING THE FRUIT:

2 large peaches

1 tablespoon lemon juice

3 tablespoons unsalted butter

¼ cup (firmly packed) light brown sugar

FOR THE CAKE BATTER:

1½ cups *unsifted* cake flour

1½ teaspoons baking powder

¼ teaspoon salt

½ teaspoon ground cinnamon

½ teaspoon freshly grated nutmeg

½ cup (1 stick) unsalted butter, softened at room temperature

½ cup granulated sugar

1 jumbo egg, at room temperature

2 teaspoons pure vanilla extract

For this cake, a circle of peach slices is placed atop a buttery brown-sugar base, then a batter flavored with ground cinnamon and freshly grated nutmeg gets poured over it all. The texture of the batter is creamy and silky, like a fluid buttercream, so it bakes into a soft, fine-grained cake. Match warm slices of cake with tall glasses of lemonade, minted lemon tea or cream-lightened iced coffee for a refreshing midsummer teatime snack.

Lightly butter an 8-inch round cake pan; set aside. Preheat the oven to 400 degrees.

Peel the peaches (dip first in simmering water, then in cold water for easier peeling); slice ¾ inch thick. Toss with lemon juice and set aside. Heat the butter and brown sugar in a small saucepan over moderately low heat until the sugar has melted down and the mixture bubbles gently. Pour into the cake pan. Arrange the peach slices on top.

Sift together the flour, baking powder, salt, cinnamon and nutmeg onto a large sheet of waxed paper. Cream the butter in the large bowl of an electric mixer on moderately high speed for 2 minutes. Add the sugar and continue beating for a minute longer. Beat in the egg, vanilla extract and almond extract. With the mixer on low speed, alternately add the sifted flour mixture in 2 additions and the milk in 1 addition, beginning and ending with flour. Spoon the batter evenly over the peaches.

½ teaspoon pure almond
extract

½ cup milk, at room
temperature

One 8-inch round cake

Bake the cake on the lower-third-level rack of the pre-heated oven for about 30 to 35 minutes, or until the cake is golden on top and a wooden pick inserted into the cake comes out clean and dry.

Let cool in the pan on a wire rack for 3 to 4 minutes. Loosen the cake by running a thin, flexible palette knife between the cake and the edge of the pan. Invert onto a shallow, lipped serving plate, fruit side up.

Serve the cake warm, cut in thick wedges.

Note: Two ripe pears, peeled and sliced, may be substituted for the peaches. Leave out the almond extract and add ½ teaspoon ground ginger with the spices.

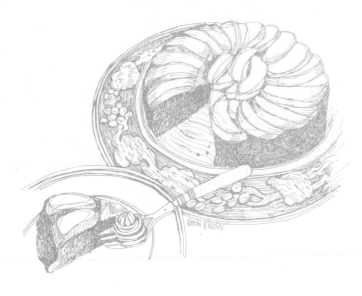

Spiced Nectarine Upside-Down Cake

This upside-down cake is light and moist, and light molasses gives it a certain depth of color and taste. Molasses and brown sugar make a good combination with spices such as ginger, cinnamon and nutmeg for cakes that feature fresh fruit like nectarines and peaches. Served with a pitcher of cold lemonade or mint-spiked tea and a bowl of sweetened whipped cream, slices of this cake will get you through the hot, sun-drenched days of summer.

❖❖❖

FOR PREPARING THE FRUIT:

2 tablespoons unsalted butter, melted

⅓ cup granulated sugar, blended with ½ teaspoon ground cinnamon

2 large or 3 small ripe nectarines, halved, pitted, and sliced ¾ inch thick, slices tossed in 1 tablespoon lemon juice

FOR THE CAKE BATTER:

1⅓ cups *sifted* all-purpose flour

½ teaspoon baking soda

¾ teaspoon ground cinnamon

¼ teaspoon ground ginger

¼ teaspoon freshly grated nutmeg

¼ teaspoon salt

Lightly butter an 8-inch round baking pan. Preheat the oven to 350 degrees. Pour the melted butter on the bottom of the pan and sprinkle evenly with cinnamon sugar. Arrange the nectarine slices over the sugar in a pleasing pattern. Set aside.

Sift the flour with the baking soda, cinnamon, ginger, nutmeg and salt onto a large sheet of waxed paper. Cream the butter and shortening in the large bowl of an electric mixer on moderately high speed for 2 minutes. Beat in the brown sugar. Blend in the vanilla, egg and molasses. With the mixer on low speed, alternately add the sifted flour mixture in 2 additions and the buttermilk in 1 addition, beginning and ending with flour. Spoon the batter evenly over the fruit.

Bake the cake on the lower-third-level rack of the preheated oven for 35 to 40 minutes, or until a wooden pick inserted in the cake comes out clean and dry and the cake pulls slightly away from the sides of the baking pan.

2 tablespoons unsalted
  butter, softened at
  room temperature
2 tablespoons shortening
¼ cup (firmly packed)
  light brown sugar
2 teaspoons pure vanilla
  extract
1 extra-large egg, at
  room temperature
⅓ cup light molasses
½ cup plus 2 tablespoons
  buttermilk, at room
  temperature

One 8-inch round cake

Let cool in the pan on a wire rack for 3 to 4 minutes. Loosen the cake by running a thin, flexible palette knife between the cake and the edges of the pan. Invert onto a shallow, lipped serving plate, fruit side up.

Serve the cake warm or tepid, cut in thick wedges.

Apple–Ginger Upside-Down Cake

FOR PREPARING THE FRUIT:

2 tablespoons unsalted butter, melted

¼ cup granulated sugar, blended with ¼ teaspoon ground ginger and ¼ teaspoon ground cinnamon

1 large tart cooking apple, peeled, cored and sliced ¼ inch thick, slices tossed in 1 tablespoon lemon juice

1 tablespoon chopped ginger preserved in syrup, well drained

FOR THE CAKE BATTER:

1⅓ cups *unsifted* all-purpose flour

¾ teaspoon baking powder

¼ teaspoon salt

Apples turn soft and satiny when cooked under a blanket of cake batter. In this cake, a spiral of apple slices sits on a bed of cinnamon-ginger sugar and butter, which get absorbed as the cake bakes. During the fall—when crisp cooking apples proliferate at farm markets, country fruit stands and food cooperatives—I make all kinds of apple desserts (pies, cobblers and cakes), as well as several different kinds of apple butter. I usually serve this cake after a brisk afternoon of leaf-gathering. Warm slices of Apple–Ginger Upside-Down Cake are delicious served together with whipped cream sweetened with apple-cider syrup or maple syrup and spiced with a dash of ground ginger.

———❖❖❖———

Lightly butter an 8-inch round baking pan. Preheat the oven to 350 degrees. Pour the melted butter on the bottom of the pan and sprinkle evenly with the cinnamon-ginger sugar. Arrange the apple slices over the sugar, overlapping them in a spiral pattern. Sprinkle the chopped ginger on top. Set aside.

Sift the flour with the baking powder, salt, ground ginger, nutmeg, cinnamon and cloves onto a large sheet of waxed paper. Cream the shortening and butter in the large bowl of an electric mixer on moderately high speed for 1 to 2 minutes. Beat in the brown sugar and vanilla. Blend in the egg and maple syrup and beat for 1 minute longer. With the mixer on low speed, alternately add the sifted flour

½ teaspoon ground
    ginger

¼ teaspoon freshly
    grated nutmeg

¼ teaspoon ground
    cinnamon

Pinch of ground cloves

3 tablespoons shortening

1 tablespoon unsalted
    butter, softened at
    room temperature

¼ cup (firmly packed)
    light brown sugar

2 teaspoons pure vanilla
    extract

1 extra-large egg, at
    room temperature

½ cup maple syrup

½ cup plus 1 tablespoon
    milk, at room
    temperature

One 8-inch round cake

mixture in 2 additions and the milk in 1 addition, beginning
and ending with the flour. Spoon the batter evenly over the
apples.

Bake the cake on the lower-third-level rack of the pre-
heated oven for 35–40 minutes, or until a wooden pick
inserted in the cake comes out clean and dry and the cake
pulls slightly away from the sides of the pan.

Let cool in the pan on a wire rack for 3 to 4 minutes.
Loosen the cake by running a thin, flexible palette knife
between the cake and edges of the pan. Invert onto a shallow, lipped serving plate, fruit side up.

Serve the cake warm, cut in thick wedges.

POUND CAKES

Wendy Wheeler

POUND CAKES

*T*he pound cakes I love to make are those spiced and flavored butter cakes that taste so good with berries, sliced fruit in season, stewed fruit compotes, a scoop or two of homemade ice cream or a hot, sweet sauce, such as lemon or chocolate. For these cakes especially, I use farm-fresh eggs from free-ranging hens; the orange-yellow yolks turn the batter a golden color and add to the rich taste of the baked cake.

My pound cakes, or keeping cakes, are made with pure extracts, the seed scrapings from vanilla beans, good baking chocolate, and fresh nuts. The batters are leavened by many eggs, as well as baking powder or baking soda or both. The baking powder and soda, I have discovered over the years, keep the batter light, even with the large amount of butter that is used to enrich the cake. I like my pound cakes to be substantial, yet fine-grained, with a tender, delicate crumb, and I have modified many of the old recipes in my file to achieve that effect.

Pound cake is a joy to have on hand in the cake-keeper, ready to be sliced and served. I think that some of my pound cakes, especially the Best Vanilla Pound Cake (page 94), Spice Pound Cake (page 102), and Cream Pound Cake (page 106), thinly sliced, also make a luxurious addition to the breakfast bread basket.

Whenever I serve pound cake, I always seem to have a bowl of fruit and some whipped cream nearby. The buttery flavor of the cake does blend nicely with the tangy, sweet-sour taste of most any kind of fruit—a mound of mixed berries, lightly poached and spiced pears, cinnamon-seasoned apple wedges sautéed in butter and moistened with spoonfuls of apple cider, or a toss of perfectly ripe sliced peaches, nectarines and plums.

A syrup spiked with citrus juice is a good thing to keep in the refrigerator for enhancing summer fruits. It goes beautifully with chunks of melon, whole berries and sliced fruit, adding a sweet, glossy finish. The syrup is simple to make and, stored in the refrigerator, remains fresh-tasting for up to six months.

Fresh Fruit Splash

To make the splash, place 1 cup water and ¾ cup granulated sugar in a small stainless steel saucepan. Cover the pan, set over low heat and cook until every last granule of sugar has dissolved. Uncover the pan, raise the heat to moderately high and bring the liquid to a boil. Boil for 10 minutes. Stir in 1 teaspoon finely grated orange peel, ½ teaspoon finely grated lemon peel, ¼ cup freshly squeezed orange juice and 2 tablespoons freshly squeezed lemon juice. Simmer for 10 minutes. Stir in ¼ cup Grand Marnier and 2 tablespoons Cointreau. Boil 1 minute, then remove from heat. Let cool to room temperature. Pour the cooled syrup into a storage container and seal tightly.

Spoon Fresh Fruit Splash over ripe peach slices and serve with slices of Best Vanilla Pound Cake (page 94); moisten a heap of red raspberries with a few tablespoons of splash and serve with thick slices of Chocolate Pound Cake (page 108); or combine blueberries, blackberries, raspberries and black raspberries with several spoonfuls of splash and serve with slices of Cream Pound Cake (page 106).

Best Vanilla Pound Cake

3 cups *unsifted* all-purpose flour

½ teaspoon baking powder

¾ teaspoon salt

1½ cups (3 sticks) unsalted butter, softened at room temperature

2¾ cups Vanilla-Scented Granulated Sugar (recipe follows)

Seed scrapings from 1 vanilla bean

5 jumbo eggs, at room temperature

1½ tablespoons pure vanilla extract

1 cup milk, at room temperature

Confectioners sugar for dusting (optional)

One 10-inch tube cake

What is more inviting than the scent of a freshly baked pound cake, pure gold and rich in eggs and butter? My finest pound cake recipe, this one, is flavored with pure vanilla extract and the seeds scraped out of a plump vanilla bean. The minuscule vanilla seeds dot the baked cake. Slices of Best Vanilla Pound Cake taste heavenly when served with poached fruit, pears or peaches for example, or with a heap of fresh berries seasoned with a little fresh fruit syrup—or with cool dips of Coconut Ice Cream (page 147). Don't forget to hide away a quarter of the pound cake to savor at breakfast, thinly sliced and lightly toasted, then slathered with jam. It's perfect with your morning coffee.

———❖❖❖———

Lightly butter and flour a plain 10-inch tube pan or a 10-inch fluted bundt pan; set aside. Preheat the oven to 325 degrees.

Resift the flour with the baking powder and salt onto a large sheet of waxed paper. Cream the butter in the large bowl of an electric mixer on moderately high speed for 3 minutes. Beat in the sugar in 3 additions, beating for 1 minute after each portion has been added. Blend in the vanilla bean scrapings. Beat on high speed for 1 to 2 minutes. With the mixer on moderate speed, beat in the eggs, one at a time, blending well after each one; scrape down the sides of the mixing bowl frequently to keep the mixture even-textured. With the mixer on low speed, alternately add the flour mixture in 3 additions and the milk in 2 additions, beginning and ending with flour. Pour and scrape the batter into the prepared pan.

Bake the cake on the lower-third-level rack of the preheated oven for 1 hour and 10 minutes to 1 hour and 15 minutes, or until golden on top and a wooden pick inserted in the middle of the cake comes out clean and dry.

Let cool in the pan on a wire rack for 10 minutes. Gently loosen the sides of the cake from the pan with a thin, flexible palette knife. Invert onto a second cooling rack, then invert again to cool right side up. Dust the top of the cake with sifted confectioners sugar, if you like.

Serve the cake cut in thin slices.

Note: To get the seeds from the bean, slash it lengthwise with a sharp paring knife, then run the tip of a teaspoon down the middle of each half to scoop out the seeds.

Vanilla-Scented Granulated Sugar

Slit 3 vanilla beans lengthwise to expose the tiny seeds. Bury the beans in 3 pounds of granulated sugar in a large glass jar. Make sure that the sugar covers the beans completely. Let the beans steep in the sugar for at least 1 week before using it to sweeten cake batters, cookie dough or ice cream mixtures. Store the sugar, covered airtight, at cool room temperature.

Grandma Lilly's Hot Milk Cake

½ cup (1 stick) unsalted butter

1 cup milk

2 cups *unsifted* cake flour

¼ teaspoon salt

4 extra-large eggs, at room temperature

2 cups granulated sugar

1 teaspoon pure vanilla extract

1 teaspoon baking powder

Confectioners sugar for dusting (optional)

One 9-inch tube cake

My grandmother was famous for this cake. She baked it every week in her Georgetown kitchen and served it with things like sweetened raspberries and strawberries, caramelized apples and pears or homemade ice cream with hot fudge sauce. As cake recipes go, the procedure for this one may strike you as strange. The method is a bit unconventional, but it does work. The milk and butter are heated to boiling hot and added almost at the end of the recipe; then, the baking powder is added all by itself. As soon as it is beaten into the batter, the whole lot is poured into the pan and rushed into the oven. What emerges is a light and buttery cake, with a fine, exceptionally moist crumb.

One word of nostalgic advice: it was always considered bad luck in our family to rattle anything in the kitchen while this cake was baking, lest it sink mysteriously. I still always leave the kitchen for the first 40 minutes, at least, of baking time. Not that I'm superstitious, of course.

———— ❖ ————

Lightly butter and flour a plain 9-inch tube pan. (Do not use a tube pan with a removable bottom; the cake batter will seep out.) Set aside. Preheat the oven to 350 degrees.

Place the butter and milk in a large saucepan and bring to the boil over moderate heat. Sift the cake flour with the salt onto a large sheet of waxed paper. Beat the eggs in the large bowl of an electric mixer on moderately high speed for 2 to 3 minutes. With the mixer on moderate speed, beat in the sugar in 3 additions, beating well after each portion is added. With the mixer on low speed, blend in the vanilla. Beat in the flour in 2 additions. When the butter and milk mixture has reached a full, rolling boil, remove it from the heat and pour it into the flour mixture as it revolves in the mixer. The beaters must be turning and the bowl moving while the milk is being added. Scrape down the sides of the mixing bowl to make an even-textured batter. Lastly, add the baking powder and beat for 1 minute at moderate speed. Quickly pour and scrape the batter into the prepared pan.

Bake the cake on the lower-third-level rack of the pre-heated oven for 1 hour, or until nicely risen and golden on top; a wooden pick inserted into the center of the cake should come out clean and dry.

Let cool in the pan on a wire rack for 5 to 6 minutes, then invert onto a second cooling rack. Invert again to cool right side up. Dust the top of the cake with sifted confectioners sugar, if you like.

Serve the cake cut in medium thick slices.

Lemon–Poppy Seed Pound Cake

2 tablespoons finely grated lemon peel

1 tablespoon pure lemon extract

3 cups *unsifted* all-purpose flour

¾ teaspoon baking soda

½ teaspoon baking powder

½ teaspoon salt

1 cup (2 sticks) unsalted butter, softened at room temperature

2 cups Lemon-Scented Granulated Sugar (recipe follows) or plain granulated sugar

3 jumbo eggs, at room temperature

2 jumbo egg yolks, at room temperature

1 cup buttermilk, at room temperature

¼ cup poppy seeds

This pound cake is tender and moist and speckled with crunchy poppy seeds that play wonderfully against the subtle lemon flavoring in the cake batter. Although I have served and enjoyed this cake for many years, I only recently added a lemon glaze. I now spoon the glaze over the top and sides of the cake while it is still oven-hot. As the cake cools and the glaze sinks in, the top and sides look faintly sugar encrusted. The glaze makes this pound cake an extra-good keeper.

Lightly butter and flour a 10-inch fluted bundt pan; set aside. Preheat the oven to 350 degrees.

Mix together the lemon peel and extract in a small bowl; set aside. Sift together the flour, baking soda, baking powder and salt onto a large sheet of waxed paper. Sift the flour mixture again. Cream the butter in the large bowl of an electric mixer on moderately high speed for 3 minutes. Add the sugar in 3 additions, beating thoroughly after each portion is added. Beat in the eggs, one at a time, blending well after each one; beat in the egg yolks. Scrape down the sides of the mixing bowl. With the mixer on low speed, alternately add the sifted flour mixture in 3 additions and the buttermilk in 2 additions, beginning and ending with the flour. Scrape down the sides of the bowl frequently as the ingredients are added to keep the batter even-textured. With the mixer on low speed, blend in the lemon peel–extract mixture and the poppy seeds. Pour and scrape the

FOR THE LEMON-SUGAR
GLAZE:

⅓ cup freshly squeezed
   lemon juice

⅓ cup Lemon-Scented
   Granulated Sugar or
   plain granulated sugar

One 10-inch bundt cake

batter into the prepared pan. Shake the pan gently from side to side to level the top of the batter.

Bake the cake on the lower-third-level rack of the preheated oven for 1 hour to 1 hour and 10 minutes, or until the top of the cake is golden and a wooden pick inserted into the center of the cake comes out clean and dry. The cake will pull away slightly from the sides of the pan when done.

Let cool in the pan on a wire rack for 5 minutes. While the cake is cooling, make the glaze. Combine the lemon juice and the Lemon-Scented Granulated Sugar in a small bowl. Invert the cake onto a second cooling rack. Spoon the glaze over the top and sides of the cake. Let cool completely.

Serve the cake cut in medium thick slices.

Lemon-Scented Granulated Sugar

Pour 2 pounds granulated sugar into a glass jar. Bury 12 to 16 strips of fresh lemon peel in the sugar and cover the jar tightly. Let the sugar stand in a cool, dark place for 1 week, then remove and discard the lemon peel. Add 8 strips of lemon peel that have been air-dried for a day at room temperature (the peel will turn slightly leathery) and bury those in the sugar. Use the sugar, without the peel, for flavoring cake batters, ice cream and mousse mixtures and in cookie dough.

Bourbon Pound Cake

3½ cups *unsifted* cake flour

1¼ teaspoons baking powder

½ teaspoon salt

1 teaspoon ground cinnamon

¾ teaspoon freshly grated nutmeg

¼ teaspoon ground allspice

¼ teaspoon ground ginger

1½ cups (3 sticks) unsalted butter, softened at room temperature

3 cups (firmly packed) light brown sugar

½ cup granulated sugar

4 jumbo eggs, at room temperature

2 jumbo egg yolks, at room temperature

¾ cup light cream, blended with 2 teaspoons pure vanilla

The crumb of this pound cake is a beautiful amber color, owing to the three cups of brown sugar that colors the batter. The faint caramel flavor is reinforced by a good slug of bourbon and tinged by a quartet of spices (cinnamon, nutmeg, allspice and ginger). I happen to love what the mingling of spices does to uplift the flavor of the cake, playing against the bourbon as they do. You can substitute rum for the bourbon, with excellent results; in that case, I'd use a good Barbados rum, like Mount Gay. A chunky fruit compote is refreshing with a slice of Bourbon Pound Cake. And paired with cool glasses of minted iced tea, slices of the pound cake make an ideal midafternoon treat.

This recipe, originally my mother's, has been through many changes in my hands. My mother used more brown sugar and less vanilla than I do, and she replaced part of the butter with shortening, but I find my proportions more appealing. This has become the version I've made at home for years.

———❖❖❖———

Lightly butter and flour a 10-inch fluted bundt pan; set aside. Preheat the oven to 350 degrees.

Resift the flour with the baking powder, salt, cinnamon, nutmeg, allspice and ginger onto a large sheet of waxed paper. Cream the butter in the large bowl of an electric mixer on moderately high speed for 3 minutes. Beat in the brown sugar in 3 additions, beating well after each portion. Beat in the granulated sugar. Beat in the eggs, one at a time,

extract, at room
temperature

¼ cup good bourbon

Confectioners sugar for
dusting (optional)

One 10-inch bundt cake

blending well after each one. Beat in the egg yolks. Scrape down the sides of the mixing bowl frequently with a rubber spatula to keep the mixture even-textured. Combine the vanilla-cream and bourbon in a small pitcher. With the mixer on low speed, alternately add the sifted dry ingredients in 3 additions and the bourbon–cream mixture in 2 additions, beginning and ending with the dry mixture. Pour and scrape the batter into the prepared baking pan. Shake the pan gently from side to side to level the top of the batter.

Bake the cake on the lower-third-level rack of the preheated oven for 1 hour and 15 minutes to 1 hour and 20 minutes, or until a wooden pick inserted in the center of the cake comes out clean and dry and the cake pulls away slightly from the edge of the pan.

Let cool in the pan on a wire rack for 3 to 4 minutes. Invert onto a second cooling rack. Dust the top of the cake with sifted confectioners sugar, if you like.

Serve the cake cut in medium thick slices.

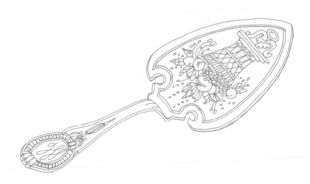

Spice Pound Cake

3 cups plus 2 table-
spoons *sifted* cake flour

2 teaspoons baking
powder

½ teaspoon baking soda

¾ teaspoon salt

2 teaspoons ground
cinnamon

1 teaspoon freshly
grated nutmeg

1 teaspoon ground
ginger

½ teaspoon ground
allspice

¼ teaspoon ground
cloves

1 cup (2 sticks) unsalted
butter, softened at
room temperature

2¾ cups superfine sugar

5 extra-large eggs, at
room temperature

2 extra-large egg yolks,
at room temperature

1 tablespoon pure
vanilla extract

This cake is a teatime favorite of many people I know. Some serve it with a hot lemon sauce, others present thin slices with raspberries and whipped cream or sugared sliced strawberries. I like the cake with a mix of sliced ripe peaches, nectarines and plums, doused in a little plum syrup to moisten the slices of fruit so that they shine on the plate.

Lightly butter and flour a plain 10-inch tube pan; set aside. Preheat the oven to 350 degrees.

Resift the flour with the baking powder, baking soda, salt, cinnamon, nutmeg, ginger, allspice and cloves onto a large sheet of waxed paper. Cream the butter in the large bowl of an electric mixer on moderately high speed for 3 minutes. Add the sugar mixture in 3 additions, beating well after each portion has been added. Beat in the eggs, one at a time, blending well after each one. Beat in the egg yolks. Scrape down the sides of the mixing bowl frequently with a rubber spatula to keep the batter even-textured. Beat in the vanilla extract. With the mixer on low speed, alternately add the sifted dry ingredients in 3 additions and the sour cream in 2 additions, beginning and ending with flour. Pour and scrape the batter into the prepared pan; shake the pan gently from side to side to level the top.

Bake the cake on the lower-third-level rack of the pre-heated oven for about 1 hour and 25 minutes to 1 hour and 30 minutes, or until a wooden pick inserted in the middle

1 cup sour cream, at
   room temperature
Confectioners sugar for
   dusting (optional)

One 10-inch tube cake

of the cake comes out clean and dry and the cake pulls slightly away from the sides of the pan.

Let cool in the pan on a wire rack for 4 to 5 minutes, then invert onto a second cooling rack. Invert again to cool right side up. Dust the top of the cake with a little sifted confectioners sugar, if you like.

Serve the cake cut in medium thick slices.

Rich Nut Pound Cake

3½ cups *unsifted* all-purpose flour

2¼ teaspoons baking powder

¾ teaspoon salt

1 teaspoon freshly grated nutmeg

¼ teaspoon ground mace

½ teaspoon ground ginger

¼ teaspoon ground allspice

1½ cups (3 sticks) unsalted butter, softened at room temperature

2 cups Vanilla-Scented Granulated Sugar (page 95)

5 jumbo eggs, at room temperature

2 jumbo egg yolks, at room temperature

1 tablespoon pure vanilla extract

The collection of nuts used for this pound cake can be varied according to what looks attractive or what kind you are willing to crack open yourself. I do prefer the way the cake tastes when freshly cracked and chopped nuts are used in the batter. I almost always make this cake at Thanksgiving, when I can buy whole nuts at the market. Because this cake is so dense and rich with nuts, it should be sliced quite thin. Serve the slices with a hot pot of lemon tea or freshly brewed coffee.

Lightly butter and flour a plain 10-inch tube pan. Line the bottom of the pan with a circle of waxed paper cut to fit; set aside. Preheat the oven to 325 degrees.

Sift together the flour, baking powder, salt, nutmeg, mace, ginger and allspice onto a large sheet of waxed paper. Cream the butter in the large bowl of an electric mixer on moderately high speed for 3 to 4 minutes. Add the sugar in 3 additions, beating thoroughly for 1 minute after each portion is added. Beat in the eggs, one at a time, blending well after each one. Beat in the egg yolks. Blend in the vanilla. With the mixer on low speed, alternately add the sifted dry ingredients in 3 additions and the milk–cream mixture in 2 additions, beginning and ending with the dry mixture. By hand, stir in the walnuts, pecans, almonds, Brazil nuts and black walnuts. Spoon the batter into the prepared pan. Shake the pan gently from side to side to level the top.

½ cup milk, blended
with ½ cup light
cream, at room
temperature

1 cup walnuts, coarsely
chopped

1 cup pecans, coarsely
chopped

½ cup blanched and
skinned almonds,
lightly toasted and
coarsely chopped

½ cup Brazil nuts,
coarsely chopped

¼ cup black walnuts,
coarsely chopped

One 10-inch tube cake

Bake the cake on the lower-third-level rack of the pre-heated oven for about 1 hour and 30 minutes to 1 hour and 40 minutes, or until a wooden pick inserted into the center of the cake comes out clean and dry and the cake pulls slightly away from the sides of the baking pan.

Cool in the pan on a wire rack for about 4 to 5 minutes, then invert onto a second cooling rack. Peel away the waxed paper if it has stuck to the bottom of the cake. Invert again to cool right side up.

Serve the cake cut in thin slices.

Cream Pound Cake

4 cups *unsifted* all-
   purpose flour

3 teaspoons baking
   powder

¾ teaspoon salt

2 cups (4 sticks) unsalted
   butter, softened at
   room temperature

3 cups Vanilla-Scented
   Granulated Sugar
   (page 95)

5 jumbo eggs, at room
   temperature

2 jumbo egg yolks, at
   room temperature

2 tablespoons pure
   vanilla extract

1 cup heavy cream,
   blended with the seed
   scrapings from 1
   vanilla bean, at room
   temperature

Confectioners sugar for
   dusting (optional)

One 10-inch tube cake

Heavy cream, plenty of eggs, butter and vanilla-flavored sugar go into this mighty pound cake. It is a fine cake to have on hand at any time of year—to serve with summer's sun-kissed berries, the mellow pears of winter (poached in wine) or ruby red strawberries in spring. I often present a Cream Pound Cake on a big flowered china plate and ring the edges with fresh lavender.

Lightly butter and flour a plain 10-inch tube pan and line the bottom of the pan with a circle of waxed paper cut to fit; set aside. Preheat the oven to 350 degrees.

Sift the flour with the baking powder and salt onto a large sheet of waxed paper. Cream the butter in the large bowl of an electric mixer on moderately high speed for 4 minutes. Beat in the sugar in 4 additions, beating for 1 minute after each portion is added. Blend in the eggs, one at a time, beating well after each one. Scrape down the sides of the mixing bowl frequently with a rubber spatula to keep the batter even-textured. Beat in the egg yolks. Blend in the vanilla extract. With the mixer on low speed, alternately add the sifted dry ingredients in 3 additions and the cream in 2 additions, beginning and ending with the dry mixture. Scrape down the sides of the mixing bowl with a rubber spatula, then blend again to ensure an even-textured batter. Pour and scrape the batter into the prepared pan. Shake the pan gently from side to side to level the top of the batter.

Bake the cake on the lower-third-level rack of the preheated oven for 1 hour to 1 hour and 15 minutes, or until the cake is golden on top and a wooden pick inserted in the center of the cake comes out clean and dry. The cake will pull slightly away from the sides of the pan when done.

Let cool in the pan on a wire rack for 4 to 5 minutes, then invert onto a second cooling rack. Peel away the waxed paper if it has stuck to the bottom of the cake. Invert again to cool right side up. Dust the top of the cake with sifted confectioners sugar, if you like.

Serve the cake cut in thin slices.

Chocolate Pound Cake

3 cups plus 2 table-
spoons *sifted* all-
purpose flour

3 teaspoons baking
powder

1 teaspoon salt

1 cup *unsifted*
unsweetened cocoa
powder

1 cup (2 sticks) unsalted
butter, softened at
room temperature

3 cups Vanilla-Scented
Granulated Sugar
(page 95)

3 jumbo eggs, at room
temperature

2 teaspoons pure vanilla
extract

2 teaspoons chocolate
extract

1½ cups milk, at room
temperature, blended
with the seed
scrapings from
1 vanilla bean

My most requested cake recipe by far, this pound cake is full of the aroma of chocolate. The batter is charged with a good shot of vanilla—in the form of vanilla extract, vanilla-flavored sugar and the seed scrapings from a vanilla bean—which enhances the flavor of the chocolate. The batter is ample, and it bakes up into a generous cake; for that reason you must use a large 10-inch tube pan. Slices of pound cake, topped off with a sprinkling of confectioners sugar, are delicious together with dips of Pure Vanilla Ice Cream (page 142) or Coconut Ice Cream (page 147).

This recipe was handed down to me from my grandmother, who liked to bake this cake on Saturday afternoon and serve it after dinner with vanilla ice cream. Everyone always came by her house for dessert on Saturday night, knowing that this cake would be freshly baked and under her stainless steel cake-keeper. I have made small changes in the original recipe, such as using vanilla sugar in place of fine granulated sugar and increasing the amount of cocoa just a bit.

———— ❖❖❖ ————

Lightly butter and flour a plain 10-inch tube pan; line the bottom of the pan with a circle of waxed paper cut to fit and butter the paper. Set aside. Preheat the oven to 325 degrees.

Resift the flour with the baking powder, salt and cocoa onto a large sheet of waxed paper. Cream the butter in the large bowl of an electric mixer on moderately high speed

¼ cup light cream, at
    room temperature
Confectioners sugar for
    dusting (optional)

One 10-inch tube cake

for 3 minutes. Beat in the sugar in 3 additions, blending well after each portion. Beat in the eggs, one a time, beating thoroughly after each one. Blend in the vanilla and chocolate extracts. With the mixer on low speed, alternately add the sifted dry ingredients in 3 additions and the milk–vanilla blend in 2 additions, beginning and ending with the dry mixture. Pour in the light cream and beat for 4 minutes on low speed. Carefully pour and scrape the batter into the prepared pan. Shake the pan gently from side to side to level the top.

Bake the cake on the lower-third-level rack of the preheated oven for 1 hour and 15 minutes to 1 hour and 30 minutes, or until the cake is well-risen and a wooden pick inserted in the center comes out clean and dry. The cake will pull slightly away from the sides of the baking pan when done.

Let cool in the pan on a wire rack for 4 to 5 minutes. Carefully invert onto a second cooling rack. Peel away the waxed paper if it has stuck to the bottom of the cake. Invert once more to cool right side up. Dust the top of the cake with a little sifted confectioners sugar, if you like.

Serve the cake cut in thick slices.

FRESH FRUIT PICNIC CAKES

1989
plum jam

Wendy Wheeler

FRESH FRUIT PICNIC CAKES

————◆◆◆————

*F*ruit cakes are simple, single-layer concoctions that taste country-fresh. Making them is a handy—and economical—way to use up just a few peaches, an apple or two, a cupful of berries or a big handful of petite blue plums. Some cakes are made from creamed batters that enclose whole berries, sliced fruit or a tangle of shredded fruit, while others are made from thick and soft buttery doughs that form a pillow-like base for a layer of cut-up fruit. These cakes are a snap to make and provide just the right sweet fillip to the end of a meal.

For traveling ease, the cakes are baked in 8- or 9-inch springform pans. A springform pan has a wide hinged band that clasps to the bottom of the cake pan. Leave the band attached while the cake is being transported, to protect it while you are on the road. When you are ready to serve dessert, just remove the band and cut the cake in wedges.

If you bake one of these fragrant cakes to serve at home, offer a flavored whipped cream to serve on the side. The whipped cream can be sweetened with fresh fruit syrup or confectioners sugar. Apple cider-scented whipped cream, for example, would make a light, creamy partner to a slice of Spicy Apple Cake (page 116). And Fresh Peach Cake (page 118) is just wonderful with a dollop of peach-flavored whipped cream. Generally, I blend 2 to 3 tablespoons of syrup into 2 cups of lightly whipped cream.

Plum Cake

1¼ cups *sifted* cake flour

¼ teaspoon baking powder

⅛ teaspoon salt

½ teaspoon ground cinnamon

¼ teaspoon freshly grated nutmeg

⅛ teaspoon ground allspice

½ cup (1 stick) unsalted butter, softened at room temperature

½ cup plus 1 tablespoon Vanilla-Scented Granulated Sugar (page 95) or plain granulated sugar

1 tablespoon (firmly packed) light brown sugar

2 teaspoons pure vanilla extract

2 jumbo eggs, at room temperature, separated

Pinch of cream of tartar

10 small fresh purple prune plums, halved, pitted and quartered

This delicately spiced cake is light and soft, with quarters of small prune plums scattered on top, helter-skelter. The cake bakes to a moist, fruity conclusion. Plum cake can be served plain or fancy, as you like, with scoops of homemade ice cream, a pitcher of custard sauce or a bowl of whipped cream. If you are picnic-bound, bring a shaker of confectioners sugar along and sprinkle a haze of it on top just before serving.

Lightly butter and flour a 9-inch round springform pan; set aside. Preheat the oven to 375 degrees.

Resift the flour with the baking powder, salt, cinnamon, nutmeg and allspice onto a large sheet of waxed paper. Beat the butter in the large bowl of an electric mixer on moderately high speed for 2 to 3 minutes. Add ½ cup of the granulated sugar and all of the brown sugar; continue beating for 1 to 2 minutes longer. Blend in the vanilla extract and egg yolks, beating well. On low speed, add the sifted dry ingredients, beating just until the particles of flour have been absorbed.

Beat the egg whites in a clean mixing bowl until frothy. Add cream of tartar and continue beating until soft peaks are formed. Sprinkle with the remaining tablespoon of granulated sugar and continue beating until firm, but not stiff, peaks are formed. Vigorously stir a quarter of the egg whites into the prepared batter, then fold in the remaining whites. Carefully spoon the batter into the prepared baking

FOR FINISHING THE CAKE:

1 tablespoon granulated sugar, blended with ⅛ teaspoon ground cinnamon

2 teaspoons unsalted butter, cut into bits

Confectioners sugar for dusting (optional)

One 9-inch round cake

pan. Place the plum quarters here and there on top of the batter, flesh side up. Sprinkle the sugar–cinnamon blend on top of the plums and dot with butter bits.

Bake the cake on the lower-third-level rack of the preheated oven for about 35 minutes, or until a wooden pick inserted into the cake comes out clean and dry (test between pieces of fruit). The cake will pull slightly away from the sides of the baking pan when done.

Let cool in the pan on a wire rack for 10 minutes, then remove the hinged ring of the pan. Let cool completely. (If you are transporting this cake to a picnic, leave the outer band on for traveling.) Dust the top of the cake with a little confectioners sugar, if you like.

Serve the cake cut in wedges.

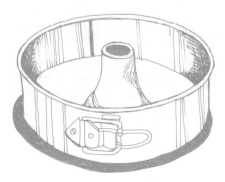

Spicy Apple Cake

1½ cups *unsifted* cake flour

1 teaspoon baking powder

½ teaspoon baking soda

¼ teaspoon salt

½ teaspoon ground cinnamon

½ teaspoon freshly grated nutmeg

¼ teaspoon ground allspice

¼ teaspoon ground ginger

⅛ teaspoon ground cloves

½ cup (1 stick) unsalted butter, softened at room temperature

¾ cup granulated sugar

3 tablespoons (firmly packed) light brown sugar

1 extra-large egg, at room temperature

2 extra-large egg yolks, at room temperature

Loaded with spices and flavored with brown sugar, this simple cake contains shreds of tart apple that keep it very moist and soft. Pack up an apple cake in the autumn picnic hamper with thermoses of hot apple cider or mulled wine.

Lightly butter and flour a 9-inch round springform pan; set aside. Preheat the oven to 350 degrees.

Sift the flour with the baking powder, baking soda, salt, cinnamon, nutmeg, allspice, ginger and cloves onto a large sheet of waxed paper. Cream the butter in the large bowl of an electric mixer on moderately high speed for 1 minute. Beat in the granulated sugar and brown sugar, and continue beating for 2 minutes. Beat in the egg. Beat in the egg yolks. Blend in the milk–vanilla mixture and beat for 1 minute. With the mixer on low speed, add the sifted flour mixture in 2 additions, beating until the particles of flour from the first portion have been absorbed before adding the next. By hand, fold in the shredded apples. Spoon the batter into the prepared pan. Using a small spatula, push about ½ inch of batter up the sides of the baking pan, to keep the batter level as it rises and bakes.

Bake the cake on the lower-third-level rack of the preheated oven for about 40 to 45 minutes, or until a wooden pick inserted in the center of the cake comes out clean and dry. The cake will pull away slightly from the edges of the pan when done.

¼ cup milk, blended
   with 2 teaspoons pure
   vanilla extract, at
   room temperature
1½ cups peeled, cored
   and shredded tart
   cooking apples
Confectioners sugar for
   dusting (optional)

One 9-inch round cake

Let cool in the pan on a wire rack for 10 minutes, then remove the hinged ring of the pan. Let cool completely. (If you are transporting this cake to a picnic, leave the outer band on for traveling.) Dust the top of the cake with a little confectioners sugar, if you like.

Serve the cake cut in wedges.

Fresh Peach Cake

2 small ripe peaches

1 tablespoon lemon juice

1½ cups *unsifted* cake flour

1½ teaspoons baking powder

¼ teaspoon salt

½ teaspoon ground cinnamon

¼ teaspoon freshly grated nutmeg

¼ teaspoon ground ginger

½ cup (1 stick) unsalted butter, softened at room temperature

½ cup less 2 tablespoons Vanilla-Scented Granulated Sugar (page 95) or plain granulated sugar

2 tablespoons (firmly packed) light brown sugar

2 extra-large egg yolks, at room temperature

This is a simple cake for busy days, when what you want is something sweet and fruity that's quickly made. Fresh peach slices are trapped in a faintly spiced batter as it rises. Peach cake makes a good dessert for a family dinner. It is a divine cake for toting to a bring-a-dish supper. I've even packed this cake to take along on a picnic that featured fried chicken and cole slaw. Delicious!

Lightly butter and flour an 8-inch round springform pan; set aside. Preheat the oven to 400 degrees.

Peel the peaches (dip first in simmering water, then in cold water for easier peeling); slice ¾ inch thick. Toss with lemon juice and set aside.

Sift together the flour, baking powder, salt, cinnamon, nutmeg and ginger onto a large sheet of waxed paper. Beat the butter in the large bowl of an electric mixer on moderately high speed for 2 minutes. Beat in the granulated sugar and brown sugar; beat for 2 minutes. Beat in the egg yolks and vanilla. With the mixer on low speed, alternately add the sifted dry ingredients in 2 additions and the milk–cream blend in 1 addition, beginning and ending with the dry mixture. Spread the batter evenly into the prepared pan. Arrange the peach slices in a pattern on top of the batter.

Bake the cake on the lower-third-level rack of the preheated oven for about 30 minutes, or until a wooden pick inserted into the center of the cake comes out without any

1 teaspoon pure vanilla
   extract

¼ cup milk, blended
   with ¼ cup light
   cream, at room
   temperature, or ½ cup
   half and half, at room
   temperature

Confectioners sugar for
   dusting (optional)

One 8-inch round cake

particles of cake batter clinging to it. The cake will pull slightly away gently from the sides of the pan when done.

Let cool in the pan on a wire rack for 10 minutes, then remove the hinged ring of the pan. Let cool completely. (If you are transporting this cake to a picnic, leave the outer band on for traveling.) Dust the top of the cake with a little confectioners sugar, if you like.

Serve the cake cut in thick wedges.

Nectarine Cake

2 cups *unsifted* all-purpose flour

½ cup granulated sugar

1 teaspoon baking powder

¼ teaspoon salt

½ teaspoon ground cinnamon

¼ teaspoon freshly grated nutmeg

¾ cup (1½ sticks) unsalted butter, cut in chunks, cold

2 tablespoons light cream, at room temperature, blended with 2 teaspoons pure vanilla extract

1 jumbo egg, at room temperature

3 small nectarines, halved, pitted and sliced ¾ inch thick, slices tossed in 1 tablespoon lemon juice

Sliced nectarines are topped here with a sugar and spice crumble. Ripe peaches, peeled and sliced the same way, would also be good to use in this cake. It is the perfect little cake to serve on a lazy summer afternoon with frosty goblets of tea or to carry along to a barbecue or other out-of-doors event.

Lightly butter and flour a 9-inch round springform pan; set aside. Preheat the oven to 400 degrees.

Thoroughly blend together the flour, sugar, baking powder, salt, cinnamon and nutmeg in a large mixing bowl. Scatter the cold chunks of butter on top and, using 2 table knives, cut the butter into the flour mixture until the pieces of butter have been reduced to pea-sized bits. With your fingertips, further reduce the butter to small flakes by reaching down into the flour mixture and crumbling it between your fingertips. Whisk together the vanilla–cream blend with the egg and pour it over the butter–flour mixture. Stir everything together to form a relatively firm batter. Spread the batter on the bottom and about 1¼ inches up the sides of the prepared baking pan, forming a shallow center.

Arrange the nectarine slices on top of the batter, right up to, but not touching, the sides. In a small bowl, crumble the sugar–spice–flour blend with the cold bits of butter and sprinkle this mixture over the nectarines.

Bake the cake on the lower-third-level rack of the pre-

FOR THE SUGAR AND SPICE TOPPING:

3 tablespoons granulated sugar, blended with 1½ tablespoons *unsifted* all-purpose flour, ½ teaspoon ground cinnamon and ¼ teaspoon freshly grated nutmeg

2 teaspoons unsalted butter, cut in bits, cold

Confectioners sugar for dusting (optional)

One 9-inch round cake

heated oven for about 30 minutes, or until the cake has risen, is a light golden color and pulls slightly away from the sides of the baking pan.

Let cool in the pan on a wire rack for 10 minutes, then remove the hinged ring of the pan. Let cool completely. (If you are transporting this cake to a picnic, leave the outer band on for traveling.) Dust the top of the cake with a little confectioners sugar, if you like.

Serve the cake cut in wedges.

Blueberry Gingerbread

1½ cups *unsifted* cake flour

1 teaspoon baking powder

¼ teaspoon baking soda

¼ teaspoon salt

2 teaspoons ground ginger

1½ teaspoons ground cinnamon

½ teaspoon freshly grated nutmeg

¼ teaspoon ground allspice

⅔ cup fresh blueberries, picked over

½ cup (1 stick) unsalted butter, softened at room temperature

½ cup plus 3 tablespoons Vanilla-Scented Granulated Sugar (page 95) or plain granulated sugar

5 tablespoons light molasses

Strongly flavored with ginger and molasses, this cake is distinctively spicy and dark, but its texture is light and soft. Fresh blueberries are folded through the batter at the last moment. If you leave out the berries, all kinds of other things can be added, such as currants or golden raisins, chopped walnuts, chopped crystallized ginger or chopped ginger preserved in syrup. This is a wonderful cake to take to a picnic because it slices into neat wedges, and it combines fruit and cake all in one dessert. If you are serving the cake at home, I'd encourage you to accompany it with little mounds of Pure Vanilla Ice Cream (page 142), Lemon Ice Cream (page 146) or unsweetened whipped cream with some thick lemon curd folded into it.

This happens to be my favorite recipe for gingerbread, and it has been in my family for years and years. My grandmother used more molasses and less sugar, and my mother used vanilla-flavored yogurt in place of sour cream. I have made my own changes: I add more cinnamon and nutmeg, use vanilla-flavored sugar and add some fruit to the batter.

———◆◆◆———

Lightly butter and flour an 8-inch round springform pan; set aside. Preheat the oven to 350 degrees.

Sift the flour with the baking powder, baking soda, salt, ginger, cinnamon, nutmeg and allspice onto a large sheet of waxed paper. Put the blueberries in a bowl and toss with 1 tablespoon of the sifted mixture.

1 extra-large egg, at
room temperature

2 extra-large egg yolks,
at room temperature

½ cup sour cream, at
room temperature

Confectioners sugar for
dusting (optional)

One 8-inch round cake

Beat the butter in the large bowl of an electric mixer on
moderately high speed for 2 minutes. Beat in the sugar;
beat for 2 minutes. Beat in the molasses. Add the egg and
beat it in; beat in the egg yolks. With the mixer on low
speed, alternately add the sifted dry ingredients in 2 additions and the sour cream in 1 addition, beginning and ending with the dry ingredients. By hand, fold in the floured
blueberries. Spoon the batter into the prepared pan. Gently
push the batter about ¾ inches up the sides of the baking
pan with a small spatula, to help the batter rise evenly as the
cake bakes.

Bake the cake on the lower-third-level rack of the pre-
heated oven for about 40 to 45 minutes, or until a wooden
pick inserted in the center of the cake comes out without
any particles of cake clinging to it. The cake will pull slightly
away from the sides of pan when done.

Let cool in the pan on a wire rack for 10 minutes, then
remove the hinged ring of the pan. Let cool completely. (If
you are transporting the cake to a picnic, leave the outer
band on for traveling.) Dust the top of the cake with a little
confectioners sugar, if you like.

Serve the cake cut in wedges.

Note: If you do not have any Vanilla-Scented Granulated
Sugar on hand, add 1 teaspoon pure vanilla extract to the
batter along with the light molasses.

LITTLE CAKES

Wendy Wheeler

LITTLE CAKES

———————◆◆◆———————

Baked in individual muffin tins, little cakes are those small cushions of cake that emerge from the oven well risen and plump. They are easy to serve —and all too easy to eat. You'll find them here in many flavors, such as vanilla, cream cheese and chocolate chip, ginger, apple, blueberry and pear. You can bake the cakes in standard muffin tins (about 2¾ inches in diameter) or make smaller tea cakes or larger, whopping Texas-size cakes; sometimes I bake the cakes in individual tins shaped like sea shells.

Except for the Cream Cheese–Chocolate Chip Cakes (page 134), which are perfect for satisfying midnight chocolate cravings and for packing up for a picnic dessert or school bake sale, all of these cakes are particularly good warm from the oven, split and served shortcake-style, with lightly sugared fresh fruit and light mounds of sweetened whipped cream. The Vanilla Cakes (page 136) taste especially luscious split and served with sweetened raspberries, a splash of raspberry syrup and whipped cream.

Chunky Apple Cakes with Pecans

2¼ cups *sifted* cake flour

¾ teaspoon baking powder

¼ teaspoon salt

½ teaspoon ground cinnamon

¼ teaspoon freshly grated nutmeg

¼ teaspoon ground allspice

½ cup vegetable oil

4 tablespoons (½ stick) unsalted butter, melted and cooled

¾ cup granulated sugar

1 extra-large egg, at room temperature

2 extra-large egg yolks, at room temperature

1½ teaspoons pure vanilla extract

1¼ cups peeled, cored and chopped tart

Chopped apples and pecans punctuate a spice-laden batter to create little cakes that taste earthy and robust. They are quickly mixed together in a bowl and as they bake, they perfume the whole house with the aroma of apples and spices. Warm apple cakes are wonderful together with apple slices that have been sautéed in butter with sugar and spices or with apple sauce made with fresh cider—and softly whipped heavy cream.

This old-time recipe comes from my grandmother's sister, Aunt Mamie, who really wasn't widely known for her baking abilities. Except for these small cakes and some outrageously delicious chiffon and angel food cakes and a few loaf cakes, Aunt Mamie rarely filled the house with sweet baking scents. For these cakes, my aunt used to crack her own pecans, so that the nutmeats would be oily and snappy-crisp—a practice I heartily recommend. On some occasions, she'd add a large handful (about ⅓ cup) of golden raisins to the batter along with the apples and pecans.

———❖———

Lightly butter and flour sixteen 2¾-inch muffin tins; set aside. Preheat the oven to 400 degrees.

Thoroughly stir together the flour, baking powder, salt, cinnamon, nutmeg and allspice in a large mixing bowl. Whisk together the oil, melted butter, sugar, eggs, egg yolks and vanilla in a medium-size bowl. Make a large well in the center of the dry ingredients, pour in the whisked mixture

cooking apples, such
as Granny Smith
¾ cup chopped pecans

About sixteen 2¾-inch cakes

and add the chopped apples and pecans. Stir everything together with a wooden spoon, using a few swift strokes (the batter should stay slightly lumpy). Fill each muffin cup two-thirds full with batter.

Bake the cakes on the lower-third-level rack of the pre-heated oven for about 20 minutes, or until a wooden pick inserted into the center of a cake comes out clean and dry.

Let the cakes stand in the tins on a wire rack for 1 minute, then remove them to a second cooling rack.

Serve the cakes warm.

Ginger Cakes

1 cup plus 1 table-
spoon *unsifted* cake
flour

¾ cup *unsifted* stone-
ground whole-wheat
flour

⅓ cup (firmly packed)
light brown sugar

⅓ cup superfine sugar

¾ teaspoon baking soda

½ teaspoon baking
powder

¼ teaspoon salt

2 teaspoons ground
ginger

2 teaspoons ground
cinnamon

¼ teaspoon ground
allspice

¼ teaspoon freshly
grated nutmeg

⅛ teaspoon ground
cloves

1 extra-large egg, at
room temperature

2 extra-large egg yolks,
at room temperature

These plump cakes are moist and full of the good taste of ginger, cinnamon, brown sugar, molasses and buttermilk. Adding whole-wheat flour to cake flour gives the cakes a subtle graham-cracker-like flavor, which I happen to love. These light cakes are marvelous warm from the oven, split in half and covered with spoonfuls of fresh fruit and clouds of whipped cream. Over the years, I've paired these cakes with nectarine slices bathed in a spiced sugar syrup, with sliced strawberries tossed in a little fresh strawberry syrup and with blueberries tossed in blueberry syrup enhanced with fresh lemon juice and bits of finely grated lemon rind.

This recipe has been through many changes over the years. I got the original recipe from the side of a bag of whole-wheat flour purchased at a mill in the Maryland countryside. (Sadly, the mill went the way of a superhighway some years ago.) Many refinements later, I've settled on the formula below.

———— ❖❖❖ ————

Lightly butter and flour fourteen 2¾-inch muffin cups; set aside. Preheat the oven to 400 degrees.

Sift together the cake flour, whole-wheat flour, brown sugar, granulated sugar, baking soda, baking powder, salt, ginger, cinnamon, allspice, nutmeg and cloves into a large mixing bowl. Whisk the whole egg, egg yolks, melted butter, buttermilk, cream, molasses and vanilla in a medium-size bowl. Pour the liquid ingredients over the flour mixture,

½ cup (1 stick) unsalted butter, melted and cooled

½ cup buttermilk, at room temperature

¼ cup heavy cream, at room temperature

3 tablespoons light molasses

2 teaspoons pure vanilla extract

2 tablespoons minced ginger preserved in syrup, well drained, or the same amount of chopped crystallized ginger

FOR FINISHING THE CAKES:

2 tablespoons granulated sugar, blended with 2 teaspoons ground ginger

---

About fourteen 2¾-inch cakes

add the minced ginger (or crystallized ginger) and stir everything together with a wooden spoon, using a few swift strokes (the batter should be slightly lumpy). Fill each muffin cup two-thirds full with batter. Sprinkle the tops with the ginger-flavored sugar.

Bake the cakes on the lower-third-level rack of the preheated oven for 15 minutes, or until a wooden pick inserted in the center of a cake comes out clean and dry.

Let the cakes stand in the tins on a wire rack for 1 minute, then remove them to a second cooling rack.

Serve the cakes warm.

Blueberry Cakes

2 cups *unsifted* all-
purpose flour

2 teaspoons baking
powder

¼ teaspoon salt

½ teaspoon ground
cinnamon

¼ teaspoon freshly
grated nutmeg

⅛ teaspoon ground
allspice

¾ cup blueberries,
picked over

7 tablespoons unsalted
butter, softened at
room temperature

⅔ cup superfine sugar

2 extra-large eggs, at
room temperature

1 teaspoon pure vanilla
extract

⅔ cup milk, at room
temperature

3 tablespoons granulated
sugar, blended with
¼ teaspoon ground
cinnamon (optional)

About twelve 2¾-inch cakes

These buttery cakes are chockablock with blueberries. The crumb is soft and cakelike, and it barely supports the fresh berries. I love warm blueberry cakes served with a ladleful of poached blueberries and a spoonful of whipped cream or vanilla custard sauce. These cakes also make good miniature tea cakes (use muffin tins about 1¾ inches in diameter). Pile the cakes in a basket and serve them with a pitcher of iced tea, lemonade or limeade.

Lightly butter and flour twelve 2¾-inch muffin tins; set aside. Preheat the oven to 400 degrees.

Sift together the flour, baking powder, cinnamon, salt, nutmeg and allspice onto a large sheet of waxed paper. Put the blueberries in a bowl and toss with 1 tablespoon of the sifted mixture. Beat the butter in the large bowl of an electric mixer on moderately high speed for 1 minute. Add the sugar and beat for 2 minutes. Blend in the eggs, one at a time, beating well after each one. Blend in the vanilla. With the mixer on low speed, alternately add the sifted flour mixture in 2 additions and the milk in 1 addition, beginning and ending with the flour. Fold in the floured blueberries. Fill each muffin cup two-thirds full with batter. If you are not going to serve the cakes with extra fruit, sprinkle the tops with cinnamon sugar just before putting the cakes in the oven to bake.

Bake the cakes on the lower-third-level rack of the preheated oven for 15 to 20 minutes, or until well risen and plump; a wooden pick inserted into the center of a cake should come out clean and dry.

Let the cakes stand in the tins on a wire rack for 1 minute, then remove them to a second cooling rack.

Serve the cakes warm.

Cream Cheese–
Chocolate Chip
Cakes

**FOR THE CHOCOLATE
BATTER:**

1½ cups *unsifted* all-
purpose flour

1 cup plus 2 table-
spoons granulated
sugar

¼ cup *unsifted*
unsweetened cocoa
powder

½ teaspoon salt

1 teaspoon baking soda

1 cup water, at room
temperature

⅓ cup vegetable oil

2 teaspoons pure vanilla
extract

2¼ teaspoons distilled
white vinegar

**FOR THE CREAM CHEESE–
CHOCOLATE CHIP TOPPING:**

1 package (8 ounces)
cream cheese,
softened at room
temperature

Everybody seems to love these dark, moist cakes. The chocolate cake provides an ample base for the rich cream cheese
and chocolate chip topping. The cheesecake-like topping
bakes right into the cake. You can bake these as tea cakes
(use miniature muffin tins that measure about 1¾ inches in
diameter) for tasty little mouthfuls to serve with fresh fruit
salad. The tea cakes are also nice for school bake sales.

Lightly butter and flour eighteen 2¾-inch muffin cups or
line them with paper liners; set aside. Preheat the oven to
350 degrees.

Sift together the flour, sugar, cocoa, salt and baking soda
into a large mixing bowl. Whisk together the water, oil,
vanilla and vinegar in a small bowl. Make a large well in the
center of the dry ingredients, pour in the liquid ingredients
and stir both together with a whisk until a batter is formed.
Fill each muffin cup a little more than half full with batter.

For the topping, beat the softened cream cheese with the
egg, sugar and vanilla in a small bowl, using a hand-held
beater. Blend well for 2 minutes, then stir in the chocolate
chips. Spoon a heaping tablespoon of topping on top of
each cup of chocolate batter.

Bake the cakes on the lower-third-level rack of the pre-
heated oven for 25 minutes, or until nicely risen; a wooden
pick inserted into the center of a cake should come out clean
and dry.

1 extra-large egg, at
room temperature

¼ cup granulated sugar

½ teaspoon vanilla
extract

½ cup miniature
semisweet chocolate
chips

About eighteen 2¾-inch
cakes

Let the cakes stand in the tins on a wire rack for 1 minute, then remove them to a second cooling rack.

Serve the cakes at room temperature.

Vanilla Cakes

2 cups *unsifted* cake flour

½ teaspoon baking soda

¼ teaspoon salt

¼ teaspoon freshly
grated nutmeg

7 tablespoons unsalted
butter, softened at
room temperature

2 tablespoons shortening

1 cup Vanilla-Scented
Granulated Sugar
(page 95)

⅔ cup sour cream,
blended with
2 teaspoons pure
vanilla extract

½ teaspoon pure lemon
extract

1 teaspoon finely grated
lemon rind

1 extra-large egg, at
room temperature

2 extra-large egg yolks,
at room temperature

My grandmother loved pound cakes in all forms, and especially in the smaller, cupcake size. This recipe for Vanilla Cakes is hers, and I have changed it only slightly—I use vanilla-flavored sugar in the batter. These cakes are reminiscent of the lightest of pound cakes; the batter, soft and velvety, bakes up with the traditional pound cake finish, a tawny brown, speckled top crust. Vanilla Cakes are absolutely delicious taken warm from the oven, split, and covered with sugared strawberries (or raspberries) and a mound of whipped cream.

Lightly butter and flour sixteen 2¾-inch muffin cups; set aside. Preheat the oven to 400 degrees.

Resift the flour with the baking soda, salt and nutmeg onto a large sheet of waxed paper. Beat the butter and shortening in the large bowl of an electric mixer on moderately high speed for 2 minutes. Add the sugar in 2 additions, beating for 1 minute after each portion is added. Blend in the sour cream–vanilla mixture, lemon extract and lemon rind. Blend in the egg, beat for 1 minute, then blend in the egg yolks. Beat for 1 minute longer, scraping down the sides of the mixing bowl to keep the batter even-textured. With the mixer on low speed, add the sifted flour mixture in 2 additions, beating just until the particles of flour have been absorbed. The batter should have a creamy, silken texture. Fill each muffin cup just over half full with

2 tablespoons Vanilla-
   Scented Granulated
   Sugar (page 95),
   blended with
   ⅛ teaspoon freshly
   grated nutmeg

About sixteen 2¾-inch cakes

batter. Sprinkle a little of the spiced sugar over the top of each cake.

Bake the cakes on the lower-third-level rack of the pre-heated oven for 20 to 22 minutes, or until well risen and plump; a wooden pick inserted into the center of a cake should come out clean and dry.

Let the cakes stand in the tins on a wire rack for 1 minute, then carefully remove them to a second cooling rack.

Serve the cakes warm or at room temperature.

Pear Cakes with Walnuts and Currants

1¾ cups *unsifted* all-purpose flour

⅓ cup granulated sugar

2 teaspoons baking powder

½ teaspoon baking soda

¼ teaspoon salt

½ teaspoon ground cinnamon

¼ teaspoon freshly grated nutmeg

⅛ teaspoon ground allspice

¾ cup buttermilk, at room temperature

⅓ cup vegetable oil

1 extra-large egg, at room temperature

1 teaspoon pure vanilla extract

¾ cup peeled, cored and diced ripe pears

½ cup chopped walnuts

¼ cup dried currants

About eleven 2¾-inch cakes

Mildly sweet and nutty, these pear cakes could be popped into the breakfast bread basket, made in miniature and served with whole poached pears or simply served warm from the oven with a mound of spiced and sweetened whipped cream.

———◆◆◆———

Lightly butter and flour eleven 2¾-inch muffin cups; set aside. Preheat the oven to 425 degrees.

Thoroughly combine the flour, sugar, baking powder, baking soda, salt, cinnamon, nutmeg and allspice in a large mixing bowl. Whisk together the buttermilk, oil, egg and vanilla in a small bowl. Make a large well in the center of the dry ingredients, pour in the whisked mixture and scatter the diced pears, walnuts and currants on top. Stir everything together with a wooden spoon, using a few swift strokes (the batter should be slightly lumpy). Fill each muffin cup two-thirds full with batter.

Bake the cakes on the lower-third-level rack of the preheated oven for 15 to 20 minutes, or until well risen; a wooden pick inserted in the center of a cake should come out clean and dry.

Let the cakes stand in the tins on a wire rack for 1 minute, then remove them to a second cooling rack.

Serve the cakes warm.

CAKE AND ICE CREAM

Wendy Wheeler

CAKE AND ICE CREAM

—◆◆◆—

*E*ven after a warming, stick-to-your-ribs meal, there's always some room left for cake and ice cream. Although good cake is certainly good all by itself, ice cream makes it even better: the cold, rich creaminess of hand-made ice cream is a cake's best friend.

These are the ice creams I've been turning out for years—vanilla, coconut (a family favorite), lemon and cinnamon. For the ice-cream base, I use a combination of milk, light cream and heavy cream, in addition to sugar and bright yellow egg yolks from free-ranging hens. The result is a silky smooth ice cream that complements a slice of cake splendidly.

The ice cream base is made in easy stages. First, you beat a scalded mixture of milk and cream together with egg yolks and sugar; then you cook the custard slowly on the stove top until it coats the back of a wooden spoon. In the second stage, you stir a goodly amount of heavy cream into the custard and place it in the refrigerator for a thorough chilling. Finally, you transform the custard into a frozen delight.

Ice cream that is made from a stirred-custard base stores nicely in the freezer for several days.

Pure Vanilla
Ice Cream

2 vanilla beans

1 cup milk

1 cup light cream

4 jumbo egg yolks, at
  room temperature

¾ cup Vanilla-Scented
  Granulated Sugar
  (page 95) or plain
  granulated sugar

Pinch of salt

2 cups heavy cream, cold

About 1 quart

Vanilla ice cream is to cake what mashed potatoes are to fried chicken—each is good on its own, but together they make a magical combination. Creamy rich Pure Vanilla Ice Cream, formed into scoops, can top fruit cakes like Peach Upside-Down Cake (page 82), Spiced Nectarine Upside-Down Cake (page 84) or Apple–Ginger Upside-Down Cake (page 86), any of the chocolate cakes, such as Fudgy Chocolate–Walnut Cake (page 76), Chocolate Pan Cake with Chocolate Fudge Frosting (page 72) or Buttermilk Chocolate Layer Cake (page 40); or a pound cake like Rich Nut Pound Cake (page 104) or Best Vanilla Pound Cake (page 94).

———❖❖❖———

Slit the vanilla beans down the center with a sharp paring knife. Place the vanilla beans, milk and light cream in a medium-size saucepan. Set the pan over moderate heat and scald the liquid; once scalded, remove from the heat and let cool for 10 minutes. Remove the vanilla beans and scrape out the seeds into the milk and cream mixture. Discard the beans.

Beat the egg yolks, sugar and salt together in a medium-size saucepan with a hand-held mixer until light and creamy, about 3 minutes. Add the milk–cream mixture in a slow, steady stream, stirring constantly. Place the saucepan over low heat and cook, stirring all the while, until a light custard is formed, about 10 to 12 minutes, or until the custard coats the back of a wooden spoon. Remove from the heat and pour into a bowl. Cool slightly. Stir in the heavy cream.

Thoroughly chill the ice cream base, covered, in the refrigerator; the base should be chilled for at least 6 hours or, preferably, overnight.

Churn the ice cream mixture in a machine, following directions supplied by the manufacturer. Turn the ice cream into a sturdy storage container, cover and freeze for at least 1 to 2 hours before serving so that it has the chance to mellow.

Cinnamon Ice Cream

6 whole cinnamon sticks

1 cup milk

1 cup light cream

4 jumbo egg yolks, at room temperature

¾ cup Vanilla-Scented Granulated Sugar (page 95), blended with 1½ teaspoons ground cinnamon

2 cups heavy cream, cold

2 teaspoons pure vanilla extract

About 1 quart

This pale tea-colored ice cream, amply flavored with cinnamon, is a delicious partner to slices of Peach Upside-Down Cake (page 82), Best Vanilla Pound Cake (page 94), Bourbon Pound Cake (page 100), Spice Pound Cake (page 102), Rich Nut Pound Cake (page 104) or Spicy Apple Cake (page 116). Baby scoops can accompany the little cakes—most notably, Chunky Apple Cakes with Pecans (page 128), Blueberry Cakes (page 132), Pear Cakes with Walnuts and Currants (page 138) or Vanilla Cakes (page 136).

———❖❖❖———

Place the whole cinnamon sticks, milk and light cream in a medium-size saucepan. Set the pan over moderate heat and scald the liquid; once scalded, remove from the heat and let cool to room temperature. Discard the cinnamon sticks.

Beat the egg yolks and cinnamon sugar together in a medium-size saucepan with a hand-held mixer until light and creamy, about 3 minutes. Slowly add the cinnamon–milk–cream mixture, stirring all the while. Place the pot over low heat and cook, stirring, until a light custard is formed, about 10 to 12 minutes, or until the custard coats the back of a wooden spoon. Remove from the heat and pour into a bowl. Cool slightly, then pour in the heavy cream and vanilla; stir well.

Thoroughly chill the ice cream base, covered, in the refrigerator; the base should be chilled for at least 6 hours or, preferably, overnight.

Churn the ice cream mixture in a machine, following directions supplied by the manufacturer. Turn the ice cream into a sturdy storage container, cover and freeze for at least 1 to 2 hours before serving so that it has the chance to mellow.

Lemon Ice Cream

1 cup milk

1 cup light cream

5 jumbo egg yolks, at
room temperature

1 cup Lemon-Scented
Granulated Sugar
(page 99) or plain
granulated sugar

3 tablespoons finely
grated lemon peel

2 teaspoons pure lemon
extract

2 cups heavy cream, cold

About 1 quart

Because lemon ice cream is creamy with a soft citrus tang, it is a good plate-mate to slices of Plum Cake (page 114) or Buttermilk Cake (page 38). Miniature scoops are great teamed up with little cakes like Ginger Cakes (page 130), Blueberry Cakes (page 132) or Vanilla Cakes (page 136).

———❖❖❖———

Place the milk and cream in a medium-size saucepan. Set the pan over moderate heat and scald the liquid; once scalded, remove from the heat and let cool to room temperature.

Beat the egg yolks, sugar and lemon peel together in a medium-size saucepan with a hand-held mixer until light and creamy, about 3 minutes. Slowly add the scalded milk-cream, stirring. Place the pan over low heat and cook, stirring, until a light custard is formed, about 10 to 12 minutes, or until the custard coats the back of a wooden spoon. Remove from the heat and pour into a bowl. Stir in the lemon extract. Cool slightly, then stir in the heavy cream.

Thoroughly chill the ice cream base, covered, in the refrigerator; the base should be chilled for at least 6 hours or, preferably, overnight.

Churn the ice cream mixture in a machine, following directions supplied by the manufacturer. Turn the ice cream into a sturdy storage container, cover and freeze for at least 1 to 2 hours so that it has the chance to mellow.

Coconut Ice Cream

1 cup canned cream of coconut

½ cup light cream

⅓ cup milk

5 jumbo egg yolks, at room temperature

¾ cup granulated sugar

Pinch of salt

2 cups heavy cream, cold

2 teaspoons pure vanilla extract, blended with 2 teaspoons coconut extract

1½ cups freshly grated coconut

About 1 quart

Homemade coconut ice cream with a fresh slice of pound cake (the vanilla, nut, spice or cream variety) tastes so good that I frequently feel compelled to bake a pound cake just because I have some coconut ice cream in the freezer. Scoops of this ice cream are sublime with most any of the pound cakes, as I've mentioned, as well as with slices of Coconut Layer Cake (page 42), Black Walnut and Chocolate Pan Cake (page 34), Chocolate Pan Cake with Chocolate Fudge Frosting (page 72), Fresh Peach Cake (page 118) and warm Vanilla Cakes (page 136).

Place the cream of coconut, light cream and milk in a medium-size saucepan, set over moderate heat, and scald the mixture. Once scalded, remove from the heat and let cool for 10 minutes.

Beat the egg yolks, sugar and salt in a medium-size saucepan with a hand-held mixer until light and creamy, about 3 minutes. Add the scalded and cooled liquid in a slow, steady stream, stirring. Place the pot over low heat and cook, stirring all the while, until a light custard is formed, about 10 to 12 minutes, or until the custard coats the back of a wooden spoon. Remove from the heat and pour into a bowl. Cool slightly, then stir in the heavy cream, the vanilla and coconut extracts and the grated coconut.

Thoroughly chill the ice cream base, covered, in the refrigerator; the base should be chilled for at least 6 hours or, preferably, overnight.

Churn the ice cream mixture in a machine, following directions supplied by the manufacturer. Turn the ice cream into a sturdy storage container, cover, and freeze for at least 1 to 2 hours so that it has the chance to mellow.

THE COUNTRY CAKE TEA PARTY

Wendy Wheeler

When I was a child, I played "having tea" in my grandmother's library with a miniature tea service made out of sterling silver and china. I'd serve my imaginary guests imaginary tea with an equally imaginary array of sweets. My grandmother would play with me for hours, then we'd bake a real cake and enjoy a real teatime. (I drank lemonade.)

Years later, I learned the pleasures of tea anew. Now I often invite over a congenial group of people for tea and sweets—a plate of little cakes, a loaf cake sliced up, a fresh fruit cake, a pound cake—and a pot of freshly made tea (or a pitcher of iced tea). I put out my adult-size china tea set, which I purchased years ago in London, with its matching cups and saucers, serving plates and cake platters. I tuck sprigs of flowers into crisp linen napkins and fill the platters and cake-stands with cakes. I mound one or two kinds of fresh berries in one bowl and whipped cream in another. Everyone has a divine time eating cake, sipping tea and exchanging bits of gossip.

For your own tea party, bake cakes of different textures and tastes; choose a fruit-based cake, a chocolate cake, a nutty cake and a spice-charged cake. Offer hot tea with a small pitcher of cream, a bowl of sugar and a plate of lemon slices. Set out the cakes attractively, using lacy doilies underneath them for a special effect, and let your guests settle down before you fill the tea pot and pour the tea. In summer you might prefer to serve a pitcher of plain or minted iced tea or an iced herbal tea. (I like to offer my own very special "house blend" iced tea, which I make with two or three different kinds of tea bags and then sweeten with a fresh fruit syrup.)

A tea party is a fine time for introducing new neighbors to the community, for visiting with old friends, getting together with colleagues or just plain relaxing. It is a welcome interlude that warms the heart and brightens the day.

Bake Sale Cakes

———◆◆◆———

Country Cakes That Use "Goods on Hand" (Basic Dairy and Pantry Staples)

———— ❖❖❖ ————

Country Cakes That Use Fresh Fruits and Vegetables

———— ❖❖❖ ————

Keeping Cakes

—◆◆◆—

Index